Getting Started with FortiGate

Simplify and protect your network using the FortiGate
network security appliance

Rosato Fabbri

Fabrizio Volpe

[PACKT] enterprise 88
PUBLISHING   professional expertise distilled

BIRMINGHAM - MUMBAI

Getting Started with FortiGate

First published: November 2013

Production Reference: 1181113

Published by Packt Publishing Ltd.

Livery Place
35 Livery Street
Birmingham B3 2PB, UK.

ISBN 978-1-78217-820-0

www.packtpub.com

Cover Image by Aniket Sawant (aniket_sawant_photography@hotmail.com)

Credits

Authors
Rosato Fabbri
Fabrizio Volpe

Reviewers
Marco Alamanni
Andreas Felder
Sebastian Knoop-Troullier

Acquisition Editor
Kevin Colaco

Commissioning Editor
Sharvari Tawde

Technical Editors
Faisal Siddiqui
Sonali S Vernekar

Project Coordinator
Sageer Parkar

Proofreader
Bernadette Watkins

Indexer
Priya Subramani

Production Coordinator
Adonia Jones

Cover Work
Adonia Jones

Foreword

I believe that technology, even the best, is only an ornament without adequate knowledge. Training is the key point in transforming high-quality technology into an excellent product. It is important to underline that only a fine product can become a market leader. But the way to leadership is not practicable without sufficient training. For these reasons, every admin guide, doc, and technical forum, if opportunely given, can help a technological solution reach and consolidate the world-wide distribution, and it is exactly with this intention that I decided to write this foreword.

The FortiGate system was born following a simple philosophy: implementing the most important network security solutions into a single device featuring the highest possible performance and the easiest graphical interface. Yet that's not enough. Also, the simplest systems need to be studied and understood. This guide can be a good starting point for anybody who wants to approach the FortiGate technology using the latest OS version (FortiOS 5.0). It can help the reader to understand what the Unified Threat Management (UTM) system is, and why it's so flexible and serviceable to consolidate the network security, especially considering that in the latest OS version, Fortinet implements a high number of new features in terms of security, control, usability, and simplicity. Remember that this is just a starter guide, and after reading this book, you can find many other documents and datasheets on Fortinet webpages.

Enjoy your reading with the hope that it can help you to improve your FortiOS 5.0 skills.

Dr. Aldo Di Mattia

Systems Engineer

CISSP

About the Authors

Rosato Fabbri, 50 years old, has been the IT Manager for Need s.r.l. for the last 10 years. The company has more than a thousand users spread across eight sites (a national headquarters in Italy and a network of remote offices abroad). Need's network is entirely based on FortiGate appliances and on secure VPNs over the Internet. Rosato used his first FortiGate in 2003 and for him it was "love at first sight". He fully used the competitive advantage of Fortinet technology, both in functionalities and in features and that advantage made Need a use case, enabling the company to gain the trust of its customers and adding a lead over competitors.

Fabrizio Volpe has worked in the Iccrea Banking Group since 2000, as Network and Systems Administrator. Since 2011 he has been awarded the Microsoft MVP on Directory Services from Microsoft, and his focus is on Windows systems, security, and unified communications. Since the year 2000 Fabrizio has delivered speeches at many events and conferences (both Italian and international). He is committed to creating content that is accessible to a wide number of people, so he often publishes content on his *Lync2013* channel on YouTube (`http://www.youtube.com/user/lync2013`), on his personal blog (`http://blog.lync2013.org`), and on SlideShare (`http://www.slideshare.net/fabriziov`). In the last year Fabrizio has published two books with Packt, *Getting Started with Microsoft Lync Server 2013* and *Instant Microsoft Forefront UAG Mobile Configuration Starter*. He has also made available a free e-book, *Microsoft Lync Server 2013: Basic Administration* in the TechNet gallery (`http://gallery.technet.microsoft.com/office/Lync-Server-2013-Basic-0a86824d`).

This work is dedicated to those who live every day with me, my family, Federico and Antonella, and to my parents.

I want to thank all the people at Packt Publishing for the opportunity to write this book and for all their great work on the long road from drafting to publishing.

I would like to express my gratitude to all the tech reviewers that have contributed with their expertise and ideas to this book.

I extend heartfelt thanks to the people at Gruppo Need (`http://www.need.it/`) for offering the hardware, infrastructure, and tech support for the labs I have used during the preparation of the book.

About the Reviewers

Marco Alamanni has professional experience working as a Linux System Administrator and Information Security Administrator in banks and financial institutions, in Italy and Peru. He holds a B.Sc in Computer Science and an M.Sc in Information Security. His interests in information technology include ethical hacking, digital forensics, malware analysis, Linux, and programming, among others. He also collaborates with IT magazines, writing articles on Linux and IT Security.

I'd like to thank my family, especially my wife and my little son, for their love and support.

Andreas Felder attended Rochester Institute of Technology and earned his Bachelor's degree in Applied Networking and System Administration as well as Information Security and Forensics. He is currently pursuing his Master's degree in Networking and System Administration. He has been working for six years as a System Administrator, with partial responsibility for the implementation and maintenance of the entire network and systems infrastructure, including several FortiGate firewalls.

Sebastian Knoop-Troullier has been firmly entrenched in the field of Information Security for over 15 years. He has more than 10 years experience in working with Fortinet products and also publishes the "Firewall Guru" blog, a real-world resource for Fortinet firewalls.

www.PacktPub.com

Support files, eBooks, discount offers and more

You might want to visit www.PacktPub.com for support files and downloads related to your book.

Did you know that Packt offers eBook versions of every book published, with PDF and ePub files available? You can upgrade to the eBook version at www.PacktPub.com and as a print book customer, you are entitled to a discount on the eBook copy. Get in touch with us at service@packtpub.com for more details.

At www.PacktPub.com, you can also read a collection of free technical articles, sign up for a range of free newsletters and receive exclusive discounts and offers on Packt books and eBooks.

http://PacktLib.PacktPub.com

Do you need instant solutions to your IT questions? PacktLib is Packt's online digital book library. Here, you can access, read and search across Packt's entire library of books.

Why Subscribe?

- Fully searchable across every book published by Packt
- Copy and paste, print and bookmark content
- On demand and accessible via web browser

Free Access for Packt account holders

If you have an account with Packt at www.PacktPub.com, you can use this to access PacktLib today and view nine entirely free books. Simply use your login credentials for immediate access.

Instant Updates on New Packt Books

Get notified! Find out when new books are published by following @PacktEnterprise on Twitter, or the *Packt Enterprise* Facebook page.

Table of Contents

Preface

Fortinet is one of the leading vendors of network security solutions in the world. Its FortiGate family of products is widely used and appreciated and includes solutions optimized for high-end, mid-range, desktop, and virtual scenarios. Such a success means that security professionals, networking experts, and system administrators often have to manage (or at least have to deal with) a FortiGate appliance. The documentation as well as training courses available on the Fortinet knowledge base are of excellent quality. Nevertheless, the first impact with a complex apparatus as the FortiGate, often creates significant difficulties. Getting started with FortiGate has the purpose of introducing the main functionality of the FortiGate appliance, using the latest release available of FortiOS (5.0). Routing, security filters, security policies, tunneling, and high availability are introduced and then demonstrated with practical configuration examples. This way the text provides the reader with an experience as close as possible to what is required in real-world scenarios.

What this book covers

Chapter 1, *First Steps*, introduces the basic administrative tools of a FortiGate administrator (web-based manager and CLI). After a quick overview of the fundamental steps we have to take for a FortiGate unit to be operational, the text explains essential concepts and procedures related to VLANs and routing.

Chapter 2, *Filters, Policies, and Endpoint Security*, explains UTM as the main topic of this chapter, as UTM includes a large part of the services we use on a FortiGate unit. The chapter will talk about security profiles, web filters, antivirus, anti-spam, and endpoint security.

Chapter 3, *VPNs and Tunnelling*, is dedicated to explaining the available kind of VPNs in a FortiGate unit, SSL, and IPSEC. VPNs enable to use inexpensive connections to create a secure channel over insecure networks.

Chapter 4, High Availability, explores the different solutions for high availability (HA) and load balancing available for FortiGate units. The text will talk about link aggregation, clustering, and VDOMs.

Chapter 5, Troubleshooting, examines the previous contents from a troubleshooting point of view. Tools to debug and correct errors related to routing, security policies, VDOMS, VPNs, and HA are explained here.

What you need for this book

A FortiGate network security appliance (physical or virtual) with FortiOS 5.0 is required to use the topics presented in the book. Some desktop class appliances will not include all the services explained in the text.

Who this book is for

Getting Started With FortiGate is a starting point when you have to administer or configure a FortiGate unit, especially if you have no previous experience. For people who have never managed a FortiGate unit, the book walks through the basic concepts and common mistakes. The book is suited to the needs of network administrators, security managers, and IT professionals.

Conventions

In this book, you will find a number of styles of text that distinguish between different kinds of information. Here are some examples of these styles, and an explanation of their meaning.

Code words in text, database table names, folder names, filenames, file extensions, pathnames, dummy URLs, user input, and Twitter handles are shown as follows: "The aforementioned administrative task requires the use of the `config vpn l2tp` command in the CLI."

Any command-line input or output is written as follows:

```
config antivirus settings | set default-db extended | end
config antivirus settings | set grayware enable | end
```

New terms and **important words** are shown in bold. Words that you see on the screen, in menus or dialog boxes for example, appear in the text like this: "The resulting data is included in the **Device definition** menu under the **Device** tab in the **User & Device** option."

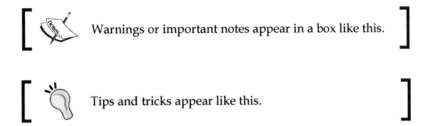

[Warnings or important notes appear in a box like this.]

[Tips and tricks appear like this.]

Reader feedback

Feedback from our readers is always welcome. Let us know what you think about this book—what you liked or may have disliked. Reader feedback is important for us to develop titles that you really get the most out of.

To send us general feedback, simply send an e-mail to feedback@packtpub.com, and mention the book title via the subject of your message.

If there is a topic that you have expertise in and you are interested in either writing or contributing to a book, see our author guide on www.packtpub.com/authors.

Customer support

Now that you are the proud owner of a Packt book, we have a number of things to help you to get the most from your purchase.

Errata

Although we have taken every care to ensure the accuracy of our content, mistakes do happen. If you find a mistake in one of our books—maybe a mistake in the text or the code—we would be grateful if you would report this to us. By doing so, you can save other readers from frustration and help us improve subsequent versions of this book. If you find any errata, please report them by visiting http://www.packtpub.com/submit-errata, selecting your book, clicking on the **errata submission form** link, and entering the details of your errata. Once your errata are verified, your submission will be accepted and the errata will be uploaded on our website, or added to any list of existing errata, under the Errata section of that title. Any existing errata can be viewed by selecting your title from http://www.packtpub.com/support.

Piracy

Piracy of copyright material on the Internet is an ongoing problem across all media. At Packt, we take the protection of our copyright and licenses very seriously. If you come across any illegal copies of our works, in any form, on the Internet, please provide us with the location address or website name immediately so that we can pursue a remedy.

Please contact us at copyright@packtpub.com with a link to the suspected pirated material.

We appreciate your help in protecting our authors, and our ability to bring you valuable content.

Questions

You can contact us at questions@packtpub.com if you are having a problem with any aspect of the book, and we will do our best to address it.

1
First Steps

Fortinet FortiGate is a line of products that includes a series of network appliances. An appliance is defined as a discrete hardware device with integrated software, optimized to give specific features. The single device integrates networking and security features to achieve what is called a **Unified Threat Management (UTM)** approach to security.

The main advantages of the UTM viewpoint are:

- Consolidation of security functions on a single device. We are not required to reiterate several times the same filters on different devices.
- Consolidated administrative interface based on a single management console.
- Consistent updates across all the devices involved in UTM.

Based on the aforementioned approach to security, a FortiGate is able to grant:

- Networking services at layer 2 and layer 3 (switching and routing, both static and dynamic)
- Network security services (firewalling, secure VPN connection, intrusion detection, and endpoint security)
- Application security services (spam and virus controls, web filtering, application control, and data leak prevention)

 Fortinet uses proprietary chipsets and a processor known as a **Content Processor (CP)** ASIC. The main advantage of this architecture is to address the performance issues that could be associated with the UTM approach. For more details see the FortiGate Hardware Guide: `http://docs.fortinet.com/fgt/handbook/40mr3/fortigate-hardware-40-mr3.pdf`.

Administering a FortiGate

We are able to manage one or all the aforementioned security features from one of the administrative tools of the device, a graphical interface (the web-based manager), and a **command line** (CLI). In the following screenshot, we can see the dashboard of the web-based manager and the CLI paired in the same screen:

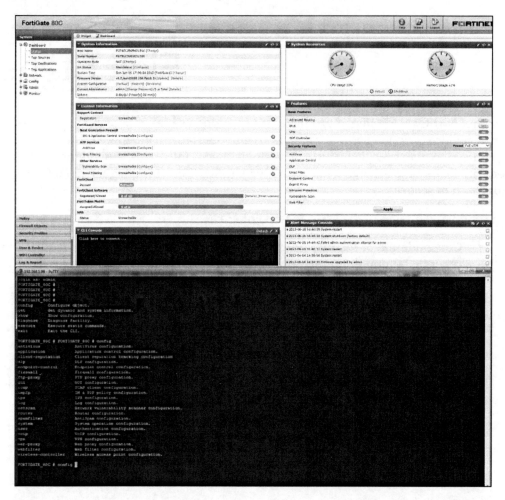

Access to the web-based manager requires a browser and an Ethernet connection between the FortiGate unit and the administrator's workstation.

The CLI can be used inside the graphical dashboard or we can detach it to use the command line in a separate window. The CLI is also the only administrative access we have when we access a FortiGate from a Telnet (or SSH) connection.

A Telnet session uses clear text in all transmissions. Everything we type during a Telnet session, including passwords, is basically readable on the network. SSH encrypts information and makes it unreadable. If we have the option to select a connection type, SSH is to be preferred over Telnet.

We are able to open the CLI from the browser as a part of the web-based manager or using a terminal connection that requires an RJ-45 to DB-9 serial cable and a terminal emulation client like PuTTY.

While the graphical interface is easier to manage and does not require knowledge of specific commands, the command line has some advantages:

- To troubleshoot problems with the operation of a FortiGate as we are able to use the `diagnose debug` command in the CLI console. This is something we will see in more detail in *Chapter 5, Troubleshooting*.

- To script and automatize operations.

- For accessing configuration items that are only available using the CLI. An example is the **FortiGate Session Life Support Protocol (FGSP)** explained in *Chapter 4, High Availability*.

- To apply modifications and changes on multiple devices in a reliable and less error prone manner.

To allow SSH access to the CLI, we have to enable this kind of administrative access on at least one interface. The operation is performed as shown in the section, *Selecting the operation mode and configuring the internal and external interfaces.*

Unboxing the FortiGate and license options

Usually the package we receive contains at least the device, a quick start guide, a power cord, a CD-ROM containing software, and an RJ-45 to DB-9 serial cable.

The software included in the box is usually older than the one we are able to download from the Internet. After the registration procedure described in this section, we can download the updated release of all the required firmware and software.

Depending on the kind of license we have purchased, the device will have some or all of the available features:

- **FortiCare**: It is the less costly option and includes hardware support and software upgrades. This license enables the use of the FortiGate as a networking device with the capability to configure intranets (also using VPNs).

- **Bundle**: This license adds updates for the UTM features like antivirus, web filtering, IPS, and anti-spam.

- **A third option**: Buying one or more single UTM features instead of the full bundle is available for medium and high end devices.

Features can be enabled or disabled based on our needs. We can also buy some features as an additional option to our license later on and activate them as soon as the new options are available. This is done using the **Features** option in the **Config** widget. The related pane is shown in the following screenshot:

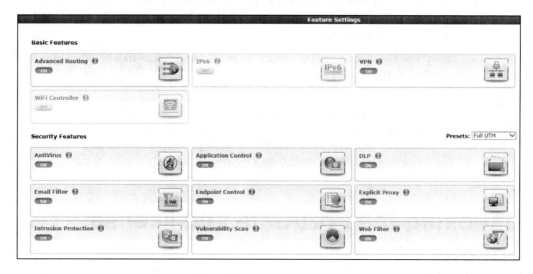

First access to a FortiGate

Depending on the model of FortiGate, we will have different number of interfaces and their disposition will change. Some models have ports labeled as Internal and External, whereas other Fortigate units will have ports labeled port1, port2, and so on. Every FortiGate unit will also have a console port (RJ45 or RS-232 on older models). The console port can be used to directly connect a workstation or terminal server for out-of-band access. An example can be seen in the following diagram, showing and RJ45 management port and WAN interfaces on a FortiGate 100D:

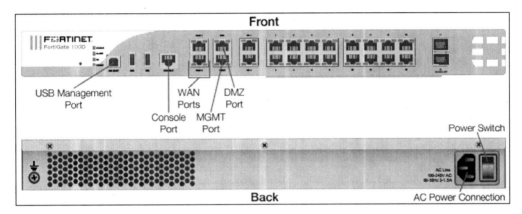

The basic configuration of a FortiGate can be performed using:

- FortiExplorer (a software for Windows and Mac dedicated to the first installation)
- The CLI through the console port
- The web-based manager

We will perform the basic configuration using the web-based manager. This requires:

- A computer configured with an IP address on the 192.168.1.0 network (with subnet mask 255.255.255.0). For example, 192.168.1.100.
- An Ethernet cable to connect the computer to one of the following interfaces (depending on the FortiGate model): internal, port1, or management.

The device should respond on the default IP address 192.168.1.99, then we can open the web-based manager with a browser using the following URL: https://192.168.1.99. The default user (admin) does not require password (see the following screenshot):

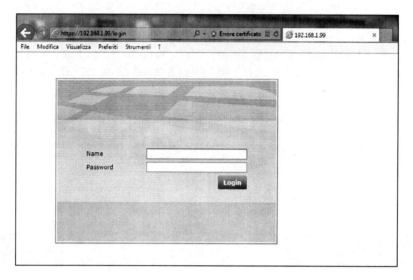

There is no mandatory order, so the following list is just a suggestion to have a checklist of things we need to do with a new FortiGate:

- Changing the:
    - ◦ Admin password
    - ◦ Name of the host
    - ◦ Time and time zone
- Selecting the operation mode and configuring the internal and external interfaces
- Registering your FortiGate
- Taking a backup of the existing configuration
- Updating the system firmware
- Updating definitions and services

Changing the admin password, name of the host, time, and time zone

From the web-based manager use the **System Information** widget (by going to **System | Dashboard | Status**). Then perform the following steps:

1. Select the **Change Password** option in the **Current Administrator** row and insert the new password.

2. Select the **Change** option in the **Host Name** row and insert the preferred name (it is a good idea to keep a naming convention that helps identifying the device location and use on our network). Note that as soon as we modify the host name, the CLI prompt will also change to reflect the new parameter.

3. Navigate to **System Time | Change | Set Time** and set the FortiGate system date and time. Select your time zone and then click on **OK**.

See the following screenshot for the aforementioned options in the **System Information** widget:

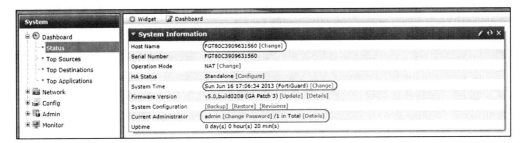

  Host Name and **Serial Number** will be required to register the unit with Fortinet. Take note of this information now to save time later.

It is worthwhile to add an **NTP (Network Time Protocol)** server to keep time synchronization for the FortiGate. We can navigate to the **System Time** options to select FortiGuard or a specific NTP source as we can see in the following screenshot:

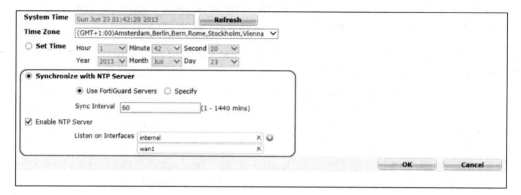

As we have just seen, a FortiGate unit can also act as an NTP server for our network (that makes sense especially if the unit is acting as a gateway between our internal network and the Internet). We have to select the interfaces that will be listening to the clients' NTP queries.

 By default, FortiOS has the **daylight savings time** (DST) configuration enabled. To disable DST when daylight saving time ends, we have to use CLI with the following commands:

```
config system global | set dst disable | end
```

Selecting the operation mode and configuring the internal and external interfaces

The FortiGate unit can run in two modes: **Network Address Translation (NAT)**/Routing mode and Transparent mode. Both the modes are explained in the following list:

- **Network Address Translation (NAT) mode**: If the FortiGate is deployed as a gateway between different networks, we have to use this mode. Each network interface will need configuration parameters. The appliance will filter the traffic and translate the network address when traffic flows from one interface to the other. This is the default mode for a FortiGate unit.

- **Transparent mode**: In this mode, all the interfaces of the FortiGate are on the same network and the appliance is not visible to the rest of the network. The FortiGate unit acts as a bridge between different network segments. The idea is to perform filtering (anti-spam, antivirus, intrusion protection, and traffic scanning) behind an existing router or firewall on a relatively simple network.

To configure the NAT mode, we need to configure a network address on our interfaces by navigating to the **System | Network | Interface** menu. Usually we need to configure at least one internal (LAN) interface and an external (WAN) interface. The following screenshot displays the configuration of a WAN interface (with a static public IP address):

Since we are talking about a public network adapter, it is advisable to remove all **Administrative Access** options (unchecking the appropriate boxes), perhaps leaving only the ping access for testing. As part of this first installation it is recommended that we also set our FortiGate to use one or more public DNS compatible with our providers or accessible from our connection. We can go to the **Network | DNS** menu and edit the server option as shown in the following screenshot:

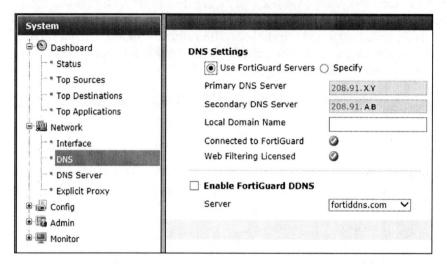

To achieve an initial connection to the Internet (or to the rest of the corporate network) we should set up a static route by going to the **Router** pane | **Static Route** option as shown in the following screenshot:

The router pane only exists in medium business and higher models. The desktop versions like the 40C model have the routing open under the **System** pane. This area under the **System** pane is only for creating static routes. All dynamic routing has to be done through the CLI for desktop models.

As mentioned earlier in this chapter, the administrative interface allows the management of different levels of operation of the FortiGate unit. A good example is the one we have just seen, with the routing layer included in the **Router** pane and not in **System** as for the previous parameters.

To configure transparent mode, we need to set a management IP address (the one we will use to administer the FortiGate unit). This makes sense because in transparent mode the appliance has no other network addresses exposed. From the web-based manager we will again use the **System Information** widget (by navigating to **System | Dashboard | Status**). In **Operation Mode** we have to click on **Change** and then select **Transparent**. We will immediately be required to add a management IP and a gateway (to make it reachable also from a different subnet). We can see the two steps in the following screenshot:

Then we will have to configure the DNS servers as we have seen for the NAT mode.

Registering your FortiGate

We should register our FortiGate at the earliest on the Fortinet support site, following the links that we can see in the following screenshot. There we are able to find all the updates related to our device and to activate the features associated with our FortiGate unit license:

As we stated earlier, host name and serial number are required to register a FortiGate unit (the information is available in the **System Information** widget).

 Registration of our first FortiGate unit will also require a one-time registration on the Fortinet website with our company information.

Updating the system firmware

Device registration entitles us to download the most recent version of the firmware (the base set of instructions stored in our device) and to apply it to our FortiGate unit. Once we have acquired an appropriate software update from the support site we can upgrade the firewall. The operation is made in the **Firmware Version** widget selecting **Update** as shown in the following screenshot:

The aforementioned widget is also used to read the current version of our firmware. We must always make a backup of the configuration of the appliance before applying any firmware update (especially if we have to work on a unit that is already operational). Backups (and restores) are performed by navigating to **System Information** | **System Configuration** | **Backup** (or **Restore**) as shown in the following screenshot:

Restoring a device

To restore a device after a faulty update, we can use the CLI from a console connection. The steps are described here: **Verifying the current firmware version and upgrading the FortiOS firmware** (http://docs.fortinet.com/cb/html/ index.html#page/FOS_Cookbook/Install-basic/update_firmware.html). For a detailed description of the CLI commands related to backup and restore use the document available at: http://docs.fortinet.com/fdb/html/fdb-user-guide/ index.html?page=source%2Freferences%2Fr_cli_admin_execute.html.

The Release Notes of the different versions of FortiOS and firmware contain a section named *Upgrade Information*. It is really important to read them because updating from one version to the other may require some intermediate steps. There could be well known issues and limits as well as information about fixed and known bugs.

Updating definitions and services

The previous steps have enabled the FortiGate unit to reach the Fortinet services and to acquire updates for all the services we are subscribed to.

It is not required to add security policies for this purpose. We can verify that the connection from the appliance to the Internet is working by pinging the name of a public site from the CLI using the command `execute ping <hostname>` (for more information see *Layer 2 and Layer 3 TCP/IP Diagnostics*, in *Chapter 5, Troubleshooting*).

The updates for the different features and licensing inside our FortiGate are unified inside a single mechanism that is called **FortiGuard**. We are able to see the status of our license registration by navigating to **Config | FortiGuard**. Services should be registered automatically and updates should be received from Fortinet by default. We can verify that the **Allow Push Update** flag is selected (see the following screenshot). In the same screen we are able to force the update process by clicking on the **Update Now** button:

All the services should show a green flag, like the ones we can see in the following the screenshot:

Support Contract			
Registration	Registered (Login ID:	) [Login Now]	⊘
Hardware	8 x 5 support (Expires: 2015-04-28)		⊘
Firmware	8 x 5 support (Expires: 2015-04-28)		⊘
Enhanced Support	8 x 5 support (Expires: 2015-04-28)		⊘
FortiGuard Subscription Services			
Next Generation Firewall			
IPS & Application Control	Valid License (Expires 2015-04-28)		⊘
IPS Definitions	4.00345 (Updated 2013-05-23 *via Manual Update*) [Update]		
IPS Engine	2.00153 (Updated 2013-05-31 *via Manual Update*)		
ATP Services			
AntiVirus	Valid License (Expires 2015-04-28)		⊘
AV Definitions	1.00000 (Updated 2012-10-17 *via Manual Update*) [Update]		
AV Engine	5.00146 (Updated 2013-05-21 *via Manual Update*)		
Web Filtering	Valid License (Expires 2015-04-27)		⊘

 If an error is shown in the aforementioned menu, probably we will have to get in touch with the Fortinet support at
http://www.fortinet.com/support/contact_support.html.

VLANs and logical interfaces

FortiGate supports the segregation (and aggregation) of network interfaces with the use of **VLAN** (**virtual LAN**). The basic idea of a VLAN is to keep the traffic of networks that we want to segregate at the physical layer (layer 2) within the same device. We are able to combine multiple logical networks on a single interface and filter traffic between them while retaining the capability. While there are different standards in order to obtain this result, Fortinet has used the international standard IEEE 802.1Q. Each Ethernet frames will have a **tag**, which indicates a single VLAN membership. Network interfaces will be able to receive data from one or more VLANs, but will discard all communications related to VLAN to which they do not belong. The traffic will pass from one VLAN to another only through layer 3 (routing) thus realizing the physical separation within networks with a single device that we talked about. To define a VLAN in a FortiGate we will navigate to the **System | Network | Interface** menu and select **Create New Interface** as shown in the following screenshot:

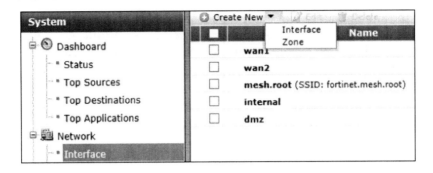

Now we can specify the network adapter to associate with this VLAN and its ID tag as we can see in the following screenshot:

 The interface will be seen as untagged if connected to an untagged device (for example, a PC) and tagged if connected to a port with VLAN enabled, like a layer 2 switch.

Repeating the aforementioned operation with a different VLAN ID, but on the same interface, we will obtain what is commonly referred to as a **trunk**. A trunk is a way to accept multiple VLANs on a single interface. This is required, for example, when we have a device (let's say a switch) for the upstream of a FortiGate, that receives tagged traffic from different VLANs and then forwards it to the Fortigate. An example is shown in the following diagram:

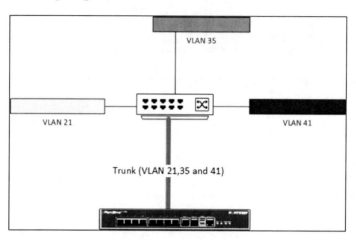

As mentioned, once the VLANs are defined, we can aggregate multiple ports into a single logical entity. Such a combination is a logical interface defined as a **software switch**.

A software switch groups physical interfaces in a software interface (also called a **softswitch**). All the interfaces in a softswitch share one IP address and become a single entry on the interface list. This method can be useful to aggregate different interfaces that are on the same subnet without creating a firewall policy. A good example for this would be combining a wired and a wireless interface so that clients on the wireless interface can see devices on the wired network. A softswitch is configured using the interface menu and selecting **Type** as **Software Switch**. The base configuration can be seen in the following screenshot:

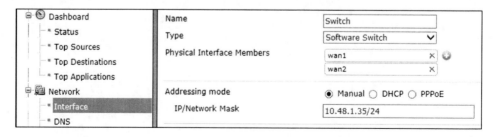

Talking about logical interfaces like the softswitch, it is also important to introduce the **Loopback Interface**. It can be generated inside the firewall and does not require a physical interface. Loopback interfaces are always up and reachable and are used, for example, to configure a unique IP for a service that is common to more than one of the networks connected to the FortiGate unit (for example, to deploy a proxy service). Loopback interfaces are also commonly used with dynamic routing. The configuration is shown in the following screenshot:

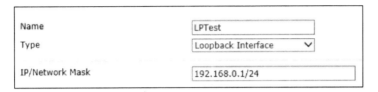

A loopback interface requires much of the same configuration options that a physical interface does. The menu used to configure an interface contains the options explained in the following screenshot:

Administrative Access					
Select the protocols available or administrative access	☐ HTTPS ☑ PING ☐ HTTP ☐ FMG-Access ☐ CAPWAP				
	☐ SSH ☐ SNMP ☐ TELNET ☐ FCT-Access ☐ Auto IPsec Request				

DHCP Server	☐ Enable	Makes the interface a DCHP server that can distribute network addresses
Security Mode	None ▾	Requires the user to authenticate with a password
Device Management		
Detect and Identify Devices	☐	
Enable Explicit Web Proxy	☐	
Listen for RADIUS Accounting Messages	☐	
Secondary IP Address	☐	Enables the interface on an additional logic network
Comments	Write a comment...	0/255

Static routing

After introducing some of the basic concepts related to the network interfaces, it is now necessary to examine the routing of data packets inside a FortiGate. Routing is the process of moving data from one network to another. The easiest method to handle routing is to create static routes that define the next step (gateway or hop) towards a given network. A gateway is a networking device that acts as an entrance to another network. It could be directly connected to the remote network or may know a route to the required network and be able to forward the packets to another gateway.

Usually we have two kinds of networks:

- **Directly connected networks**: The appliance will use the connected network interface as gateway (no explicit route is required).

- **Remote networks**: A gateway is required and it must be on the same subnet of the FortiGate interface from which the traffic is exiting.

Static routes can be configured by navigating to the **Router | Static | Static Route** menu. In the following screenshot we can see a default route that will send all the traffic to networks with no specific route to the default gateway (**192.168.1.1** in our example):

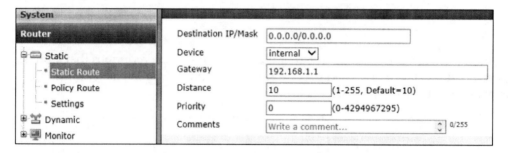

Two parameters require additional explanation: Distance and Priority.

Talking about static routing, distance is typically used as an indicator of the quality of a connection. A connection of 100 Mbps will have a distance lower than an ISDN connection. So, if you have two routes to the same destination but with different costs, the lower cost route will be used. The distance can be a value between 0 and 255.

In case we will also use dynamic routing protocols, the dynamically received routes will have their own default administrative distance. In this scenario, not all values will be available. This topic will be addressed in the section *Dynamic Routing*.

If we have two connections of equal quality (equal distance) but we want to use one of the two, we can adjust the "priority" parameter. The route with the lower priority is considered preferable and will be used. Priority can be a value between 0 and 4,294,967,295.

The workload is automatically balanced on two or more routes having equal distance and priority.

One of the limitations of static routing is the inability to detect network changes and network failures. For example, a backup route (inserted with higher cost) will never be used, unless the link status of the physical interface with the lower cost route is in a status of "link down". Even for load balancing, if the interfaces are seen as "link up", the packets are sent to both, even if the gateway of one of the two is not reachable. We will talk about interface monitoring in the section *FortiGate Cluster Protocol (FGCP)* in *Chapter 4, High Availability*.

Policy routing

The policy routing feature allows us to force the traffic on a route different from the static route that we use for a certain destination network. Policy routing is based on a series of parameters such as protocol used, source network, and the input interface of the network traffic. Policy routing adds a lot of flexibility, allowing, for example, to select and direct requests to specific service networks dedicated only to specific functions. The configuration is made by navigating to the **Router | Static | Policy Route** menu as shown in the following screenshot:

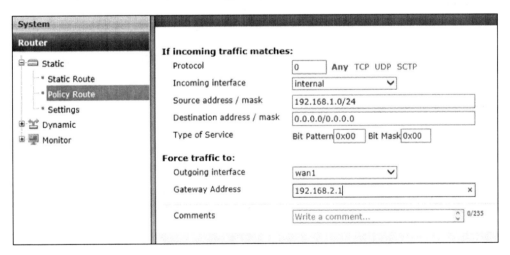

Two of the fields that we can see in the preceding screenshot require additional explanation:

- **Protocol**: Protocol numbers are based on the RFC 5237. You can read a complete list at `http://www.iana.org/assignments/protocol-numbers/protocol-numbers.xhtml`. Frequently used protocol numbers are 1 (ICMP), 6 (TCP), and 17 (UDP).

- **Type of Service**: Type of service (TOS) is an 8-bit field in the IP header that enables you to determine how the IP datagram should be delivered, with qualities such as delay, priority, reliability, and minimum cost. You can read more details in the document *Advanced Routing* available at `http://docs.fortinet.com/fgt/handbook/50/fortigate-advanced-routing-50.pdf`.

Every time you create a policy route, it is added to the bottom of the routing table. The routes and routing policies are applied from top to bottom and the first match is applied. To change the position of a policy route in the table, go to **Router | Static | Policy Route** and select the **Move To** option for the policy route we want to move, as shown in the following screenshot:

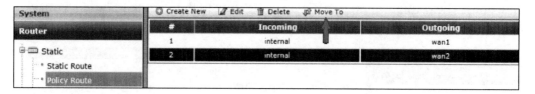

Dynamic routing

Unlike static routing, dynamic routing is based on information exchanged between network devices to select the best available route to a certain destination. This adds scalability and adaptability that does not exist in static routing. Dynamic routing uses one or more **Routing Protocols** that create, maintain, and update the dynamic routing table. The logic and the algorithms used vary from one protocol to the other and in every scenario there is one or more routing protocol that better fits to the networking needs. The protocol that we will select depends on a number of factors. Before we can compare the different protocols with each other it is necessary to introduce three basic concepts: convergence, technology used to calculate the best route, and protocol support for **Classless Inter-Domain Routing** (CIDR). The concepts are explained in the following list:

- **Convergence**: Each routing protocol has a different method to update the routing table. This will affect the time to converge the routing tables.

- **Technology**: The two main methods are **Distance Vector** and **Link-State**. Distance vector protocols use a distance value that is based on the number of hops (devices along the path) to the destination. Distance vector protocols usually send the whole routing table to their neighbors as soon as there is an update. Link-state protocols use information sent from all the connected devices and are related only to the directly connected networks. Link-state protocols also take into account other factors when making routing decisions such as bandwidth. The routing information is sent in incremental form.

- **Support for CIDR**: Routing protocols include classful protocols that do not send subnet mask information with their routing updates. With the other kind (classless routing) a series of addresses can be combined into one entry also because subnet mask information is transmitted.

The following table contains a comparison of three widespread routing protocols: RIP, OSPF, and BGP.

Protocol	RIP (v2)	OSPF	BGP
Technology	Distance Vector	Link-state	Distance vector (path vector)
CIDR	Yes	Yes	Yes
Update	30 seconds plus triggered	30 minutes plus triggered	Triggered
Metric	Hop	Cost	Path attributes
Scalability	15 hops	Around 50 routers per area, a few hundred areas	Thousands of routers

Routing protocols are also divided into two categories that determine the most suitable use scenario:

- **Exterior routing protocols**: Best used to distribute routes between different companies or organizations (BGP).

- **Interior routing protocols**: Designed to distribute routes inside a single organization (RIP and OSPF).

Each of the protocols listed has its own method of operation. RIP is less complex to manage, but due to its characteristics, it can be considered suitable only for networks of very small dimensions. OSPF and BGP are more complex but will give a much greater scalability. Being the most commonly used protocol, OSPF will be the routing protocol explained in the text.

Introducing OSPF

Open Shortest Path First (OSPF) is an Interior Gateway Routing Protocol and uses the concept of **Autonomous Systems (AS)**. AS is either a single network or a group of networks controlled by a common network administrator (or organization). Each router has an identical database that includes information on:

- The single router
- The current state of a router
- The state of the router's interfaces
- Reachable neighbors

The aforementioned database is called **Link State Database (LSDB)** and is built on each OSPF router receiving **LSA (Link-state advertisement,** the base communication of the router's local routing topology) from every other router in the same AS. To keep track of LSAs in the LSDB, each router is assigned a router ID. It is a 32-bit dotted decimal number that is unique to the AS. The router ID identifies the router in the AS and usually is the largest or smallest IP address assigned to the router. IP addresses are unique so this convention ensures that the OSPF router IDs are also unique.

To minimize the routing traffic and the amount of information required, OSPF allows to group networks into a set, called an **area** (identified through a 32-bit area ID expressed in dotted decimal notation). The topology of an area is hidden from the rest of the autonomous system. Routing takes place on two levels, entirely within an area (**intra-area routing**) or in another area (**inter-area routing**). To link together multiple areas and to allow inter-area routing, OSPF uses the concept of **Backbone**. An OSPF backbone is made by routers linking the other areas (that is, all the areas must have a direct or virtual connection to the backbone). Such connections are maintained by an interconnecting router, known as **Area Border Router (ABR)**. An ABR maintains separate link state databases for each area it serves and maintains summarized routes for all areas in the network. An OSPF internetwork always has at least one backbone area. The backbone has the reserved area ID of 0.0.0.0 (and is also known as area 0). Inter-area traffic is routed to the backbone, then to the destination area, and finally to the destination host. Routers on the backbone also advertise the summarized routes within their areas to the other routers on the backbone.

A router configured with the OSPF protocol tries to find its neighbors (other routers using OSPF, connected to the same subnet, and that are part of the same area). As soon as their LSDB is synchronized, the two routers are said to be adjacent. Routing protocol packets are only passed between adjacent routers.

The last aspect to be discussed is that when routers are connected to the same broadcast segment (for example, same VLAN on the same switch) only one router maintains adjacencies with all other routers on the segment. This is the **Designated Router (DR)**. Having a single router do all this reduces the network traffic and collisions. For redundancy purposes a **Backup Designated Router (BDR)** is also elected. An election chooses the DR and BDR from all the available routers. The election is based on the priority setting of the routers and (to resolve any tie) the router with the highest router ID is elected. We are able to configure the priority value so that a router is always or never elected (highest priority will always win on lowest values).

Configuring OSPF on a FortiGate

On each router that uses OSPF we will have to configure:

- Router ID
- Area
- Network
- Interfaces

OSPF router ID

Navigate to the **Router | Dynamic | OSPF** pane, router ID is defined here as we can see in the following screenshot:

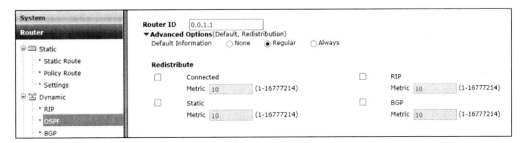

The advanced options enable the router to redistribute directly connected networks, static routes configured on the device, and information coming from other routing process (RIP and BGP) using the OSPF routing updates. The metric of the aforementioned routes can be changed from the default value.

The redistribution of routes, at this level, is not selective, but works on an entire category (for example, re-transmit all the routes directly connected to the router). We'll probably filter some routes using **access lists (ACLs)**. An ACL is a list of rules that are applied from the top of the list. Each rule in an access list consists of an IP address, a subnet mask, and an action (permit or deny). If no matching rule is found, the default action is always a deny. The ACLs are configured from the CLI with the `config router access-list` command. A more detailed explanation can be found in the FortiOS CLI Reference for FortiOS 5.0 at `http://docs.fortinet.com/fgt/handbook/50/fortigate-cli-50.pdf`.

OSPF area

In the aforementioned OSPF pane we are able to create one or more OSPF areas. The configuration screen is shown in the following screenshot:

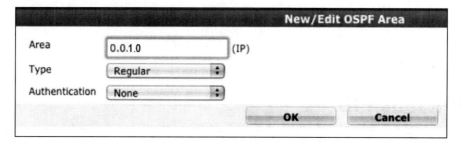

An OSPF area can be a:

- **Backbone Area (Area 0)**: This area is always required and is used to link together different areas. Sometimes this is the only OSPF area used.

- **Not-So-Stubby-Area (NSSA)**: Propagates external (not OSPF) routers presenting them to the other router as OSPF members.

- **Stub Area**: Stub area can contain a single entry and exit point (a single ABR), or multiple ABRs when any of the ABRs can be used to reach external route destinations.

- **Regular Area**: Area can be connected to the backbone by physical or virtual link. Regular area can contain both internal and external routes.

All OSPF packet traffic is authenticated and we have three options:

- **Null Authentication**: There is no authentication being used (none option).

- **Simple Password Authentication**: We will use a plain text string. It is not a strong form of security because passwords are exchanged in clear text on the network.

- **Cryptographic Authentication**: Use a shared secret key based on the open MD5 (**Message Digest type 5**) standard encryption to authenticate all router traffic on a network.

Network

Here we will add all the networks that we want to communicate on OSPF and the area to which they will be associated, as shown in the following screenshot:

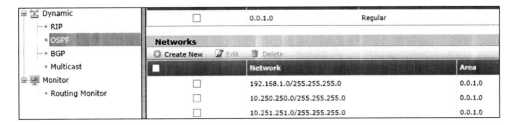

Interfaces

We must define the interfaces that will participate in the OSPF process by exchanging information. The operation takes place (again) in the OSPF pane.

Monitoring OSPF routes

By default, all routes are displayed in the routing monitor list. When the OSPF process is active, we can see the route received by navigating to the **Router | Monitor | Routing Monitor** pane, as we can see in the following screenshot:

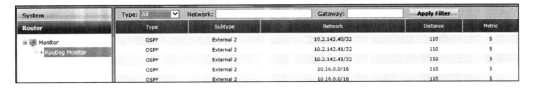

The **Type** column indicates the way we learned a route to a specific network (shown in the **Network** column). The administrative distance will decide the preferred route if more than one route is available for a destination network, while the **Metric** value will be used to select the best route among the ones known through a specific routing protocol. For OSPF there is an additional parameter, **Subtype**. The subtype field shows a value equal to **External** if the route is from outside of the AS. If the route is received from a not-so-stubby area, the value would be (**OSPF NSSA**).

Summary

In this chapter, we learnt some basic concepts and fundamental tools for management of a FortiGate. We also deep dived into VLANing and routing covering OSPF in particular. In the next chapter we will talk about Fortinet's approach to UTM, including FortiClient and FortiGuard. We will also look into web filters, antivirus, antispam, and endpoint security.

2

Filters, Policies, and Endpoint Security

After considering the FortiGate routing features, it is necessary to discuss its firewall functionalities. All the traffic that is received on a unit is analyzed using the **Security Policies**. As soon as a data packet is received, the firewall analyzes its source address, its destination address, and the kind of service it is related to. Based on this information, FortiGate tries to locate a matching security policy. If a match is found, the instructions contained in the policy are applied (while a data packet with no matching policy is dropped by default). The basic option available in the security policy is to accept or deny data packets. However, additional operations are available such as logging or UTM inspection.

Processing a data packet inside a FortiGate

The checks performed by a Fortigate unit can be summarized in four different levels of control. If any step inside the different layers containing a blocking rule is met, the data package would be discarded. These levels are as follows:

- **Ingress**: Ingress filtering controls the incoming traffic to protect the network from security risks. Controls related to **DOS (Denial of service)**, **IPSEC** (IP Security) destination, and routing are performed at the Ingress level.

- **Stateful Inspection engine**: Stateful inspection enables the FortiGate firewall to maintain context with active sessions. If a packet is a part of an existing session, the packet will traverse the device with no additional control. If a packet does not match an existing connection, it will be evaluated according to the firewall rules. The Stateful Inspection engine includes **user authentication**, **traffic shaping**, **session tracking**, and **policy lookup**.

- **UTM scanning**: FortiGate units are pre-configured with the so-called UTM **profiles**. The UTM security profiles include **antivirus, web filtering, Intrusion Protection (IPS), email filtering,** and **Data Leak Prevention (DLP)**. FortiGate units are pre-configured with several default UTM profiles, so we are able to use the default profiles or create custom profiles to match our company's needs.

 We can use the *Factory default content profiles* information of our FortiGate to find out more about the default profile available for a specific model.

- **Egress**: Egress is performed on existing data packets from the FortiGate unit. This kind of filtering can help contain **botnet** activities and performs security checks both on **NAT sources** and **IPSEC and routing**. Also maximum bandwidth-use limits are enforced at the egress level. The following diagram shows a schema containing all these steps:

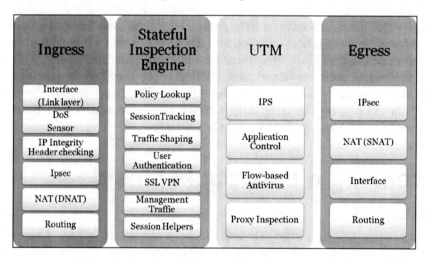

Depending on the security configuration and UTM settings, a packet could flow directly from the Stateful Inspection engine to the Egress layer.

 Inside the UTM layer, the **Proxy Inspection** is an optional step that contains **VoIP Inspection, Antivirus, Internet Content Adaptation Protocol (ICAP), Web Filter, Email Filter,** and **Data Leak Prevention** controls. During this chapter, we will focus on the Stateful Inspection engine and on the UTM layers.

Firewall features

The primary use of a FortiGate unit is to protect our networks from attacks with its firewall features. The security policies will define the allowed network traffic. Now, let's us take a look at a set of base objects that we will use to create and manage the policies.

Interfaces and zones

We have talked about interfaces in *Chapter 1, First Steps*. The firewall is able to operate both on physical and on virtual interfaces, including **wireless interfaces**, VLANS, and **Virtual Domain (VDOM)** links.

 VDOMs are a logical division of a single FortiGate unit into two or more virtual units that are independent from each other. We will talk about them in *Chapter 4, High Availability*.

There is a firewall interface that will receive the network traffic and an interface from which the aforementioned traffic will flow out of the device. We are able to establish a "direction" in which data is moving. This is the basic type of firewall control, and we can combine multiple interfaces (including physical ones and virtual ones like VLANs and VPN tunnels) into a **Zone**. The idea is to avoid the duplication of policies by grouping interfaces that require the same security policies for incoming and outgoing traffic. To create zones navigate to **System | Network | Interfaces**, inside which you click on the **Create New** option and select **Zone** from the drop-down menu, as shown in the following screenshot:

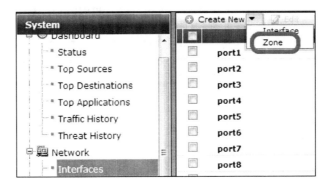

Now we are able to use a single policy with a zone as the source and another zone as the destination, rather than a policy for each interface.

> In the zone configuration, we can select the **Block intra-zone traffic** option to prohibit the different interfaces in the same zone to talk to each other. In this scenario, if we need to enable interfaces in the same zone to talk to each other, we will have to create an explicit "allow" rule using the same source and destination zone.

Firewall objects

A FortiGate unit allows us to define **firewall objects**. The objects are reusable and we have the capability to combine them, and to configure policies employing the same object more than once. The object categories include **Addresses**, **Services**, and **Schedule**, as you can see in the following screenshot:

Addresses

An address object can comprise a single IP address, an IP range, or a **Fully Qualified Domain Name** (FQDN). The use of an FQDN is useful to create rules for Internet servers and to manage policies in a large network environment, because the rules will always be up to date as long as the DNS server is able to correctly resolve the host name. To add a new address, we have to navigate to the **Firewall Objects | Address | Address** menu and click on **New** to get a screen as follows:

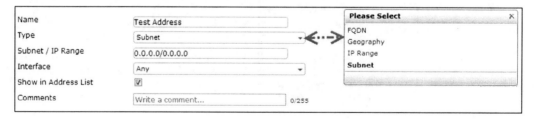

It is required to specify the interface that is associated with the address we are going to configure. The **Any** option is to be used if the address is reachable on more than one interface. A FortiGate unit also has the capability to group previously defined Address objects to keep our policies as simple as possible, avoiding rules duplication. Groups are created by navigating to the **Firewall Objects | Address | Group** menu and clicking on **New** to get a screen as follows:

More advanced addressing types, such as **geography based addressing** and **wildcards** (crated using a dedicated netmask) are also supported. More information is available in the following document: FortiOS Handbook - *Firewall for FortiOS 5.0* at
`http://docs.fortinet.com/fgt/handbook/50/fortigate-firewall-50.pdf`.

Services

At this point of the text, our control of the network traffic has been limited to methods such as creation of VLANs and filters based on the source and destination address. The TCP/IP protocol is made up of different layers; each specialized in a specific task. Inside each layer we have one or more protocols dedicated to granting specific features. In the following diagram, we can see a simplified schema with a base explanation of the TCP/IP protocols stack. The filters are limited to the **Internet Layer**.

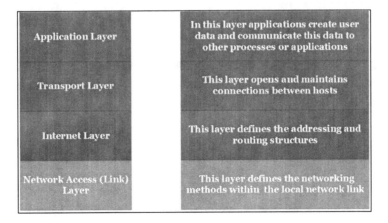

Defining services allows us to apply controls based on the protocols used in the **Transport Layer**. For every connection there will be a 16 bit number called a **port** that identifies a specific kind of service. The list of services that we are able to control includes:

- **Transmission Control Protocol (TCP)**: It is a reliable network service, which provides acknowledgment after successful delivery of data. It includes the `repeat request` functions which check whether all the data is correctly transmitted.

- **User Datagram Protocol (UDP)**: It is a service that does not require handshake (prior generation of a session) and does not check for transmission errors. UDP prioritizes speed over reliability, delegating controls to the application layer.

- **Stream Control Transmission Protocol (SCTP)**: It provides features similar to UDP (it is datagram orientated) with sequential transport of data like TCP.

- **ICMP (Internet Control Message Protocol)**: It is a part of the Internet Protocol layer and is mainly used to diagnose and troubleshoot connection errors. ICMP uses a value known as type to distinguish the different messages.

 The information provided so far is functional to the explanation of the features of FortiGate. To find out more about the TCP/IP protocol, a simple search on a search engine will provide a considerable amount of free resources.

A FortiGate firewall contains a list of default services, and by using them we are able to manage the most common scenarios. However, in most cases we will likely need to define custom services to accommodate our particular requirements. In such a scenario we are able to define a **custom service** by navigating to the **Firewall Objects | Services | Create New** drop-down menu and selecting **Custom Service**. The configuration screen is shown in the following screenshot:

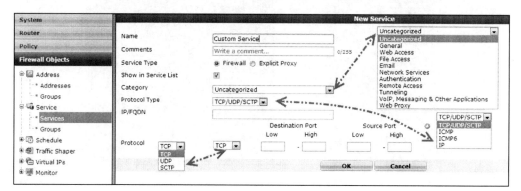

A **group** screen is available so that different services can be grouped together. This way we can enable or disable multiple services using a single policy. Groups are managed by navigating to the **Firewall Objects | Service | Groups** pane. In the following screenshot, we can see the configuration screen for a new group:

Schedules

A FortiGate firewall policy also requires us to explicitly set a time frame in which the rule will be active. The default value is **Always** (meaning always active). The two types of schedules supported by FortiGate are as follows:

- **Recurring**: This enables us to activate the rule on a specific day of the week, on a specific range of days, and so on
- **One-time**: This is usually applied to test policies or to policies that we want to make effective on demand for a limited number of occurrences

To give a real world example, some companies have a less restrictive policy during lunch time. We are able to create a policy dedicated to opening social networks and we will have to pair it with a schedule like the one we can see in the following screenshot:

By leveraging the objects that we have defined up to now (or defining new ones on request), we are able to generate one or more firewall policies. The policies are managed in the **Policy | Policy | Policy** pane. In the next screenshot, we have the **New Policy** configuration screen:

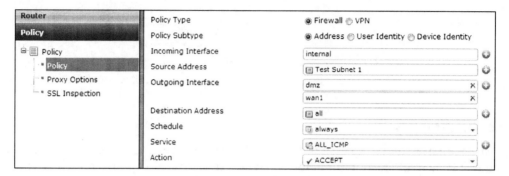

 In the screen dedicated to policy definition, we have to select an interface. If we select an interface different from **Any** in the drop-down menu, only objects connected to the specified interface will be available to configure a policy.

UTM profiles

Unified Threat Management (UTM) creates additional control layers that examine the **contents** of the network traffic already permitted by the rules related to addresses, services, and schedules as mentioned previously. The UTM options can be grouped into a **profile** that we are able to apply to one or more firewall policies. In the following screenshot, we have the UTM menu of a FortiGate unit with the different UTM features shown.

Antivirus

The Antivirus filter examines network traffic for viruses, worms, Trojans, and malware. The antivirus scan engine has a **database of virus signatures** that it uses to identify security risks. Depending on the FortiGate unit we are able to select between a **regular virus database**, an **extended** version containing "**viruses that are no longer seen in recent virus studies**," and an **extreme** version that is able to filter viruses that have been dormant for a long period and that rely on older hardware and software. There is also an option to check for **Grayware** (applications or files not classified as viruses that may still negatively affect the computer's performance). The antivirus database and Grayware options can be changed using the CLI as follows:

```
config antivirus settings | set default-db extended | end
config antivirus settings | set grayware enable | end
```

The result is shown in the following screenshot:

```
FortiGate-VM64 # config antivirus settings

FortiGate-VM64 (settings) # set default-db extended

FortiGate-VM64 (settings) # set grayware enable
```

> For more information on the `config antivirus` command, please refer to *FortiOS*.
>
> The CLI Reference for *FortiOS 5.0* is at
> `http://docs.fortinet.com/fgt/handbook/50/fortigate-cli-50.pdf`.

The most reliable method to scan for viruses is for the firewall to download an entire file and scan it once the transmission is complete. A replacement message will be sent if the file is infected. The client will have to wait untill the antivirus scanning is completed. However, for large files, this could imply a long waiting time and the user could try to restart the download. To avoid such a scenario, FortiGate has a feature known as **client comforting** that slowly transfers the file in parts to keep the download "active" on the client side. As soon as the antivirus check is complete, the user will receive the complete file or the download will be interrupted if the file is infected by a virus.

Client comforting can be configured by navigating to the **Policy | Policy | Proxy Options** pane that we can see in the following screenshot:

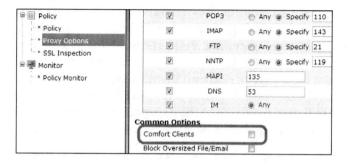

The antivirus profiles are configurations that we are able to apply in a firewall policy and define what the antivirus will control and how the antivirus engine will manage security risks. Antivirus profiles are managed by navigating to the **Security Profiles | Antivirus | Profile** menu. In the following screenshot we are able to see the configuration screen for a new antivirus profile:

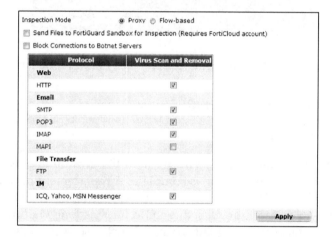

Intrusion protection

The FortiGate **Intrusion Protection System (IPS)** monitors both network traffic and system activities for signs of malicious activities, protecting the network from protocol and application based attacks. IPS requires the following two configurations:

- A security policy to define the kind of network traffic we are going to control
- An **IPS sensor**, that is a configuration to specify the signatures we want to use in a specific scenario (it is really resource intensive to enable all the existing checks together)

The steps required to define intrusion protection are as follows:

1. Create an IPS sensor by navigating to the **Security Profiles | Intrusion Protection | IPS Sensor** menu as we can see in the following screenshot:

2. Add filters and signatures to the sensor. This step requires creating one or more filters, or using an existing signature, as shown in the following screenshot:

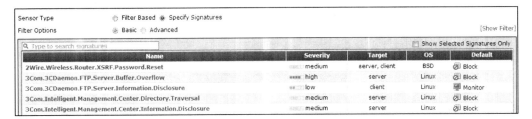

3. Inside a filter we are able to specify IPS parameters such as the OS we want to control, the protocol, the application that we will check for threats, and so on. Note that, for every signature there is a default action that we can override to create a filter tailored to our needs. The screen to configure an IPS filter is as follows:

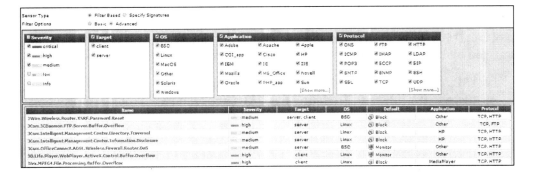

4. Now, we have to select a security policy (by navigating to the **Policy | Policy | Policy** menu) , turn on IPS, and choose the IPS sensor from the list using the menu shown in the following screenshot

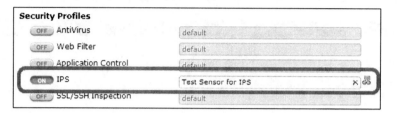

Web filter

Web filtering is used to control the type of content (websites) that our users are able to access over the http and https protocols on the Internet. The menu dedicated to this kind of control is the **Web Filter** pane under the **Security Profiles** menu that we can see in the following screenshot:

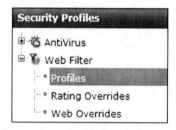

The range of threats that web filters should cover is larger than blocking malware and includes controls used to prevent problems such as exposure of confidential information and avoiding legal issues due to illegitimate use of Internet resources. To obtain this type of protection, there are the following five levels of screening, all managed by navigating to the **Security Profiles | Web Filter | Profile** menu:

1. **URL filtering:** We can block access to specific URLs or public IPS by adding them to the filter list. To define the URLs, the web-based interface provides a dedicated page that allows us to add filters and permits us to specify a path inside a website or to filter a wider range of URLs using wildcards (the page is shown in the following screenshot). **Regular expressions (Regex)** are supported too.

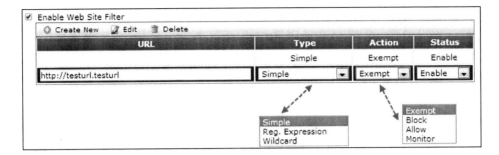

2. **FortiGuard web filter**: This is a subscription service that classifies billions of webpages to make it easier to allow or block whole categories of websites. The FortiGuard filters have to be enabled inside a profile as shown in the following screenshot:

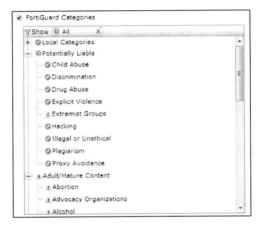

3. **Web content filtering**: This blocks webpages containing specific words or phrases (including support for patterns, wild cards, and regular expressions based on **Perl**).

4. **Web script filtering**: We can configure the FortiGate unit to block Java applets, cookies, and ActiveX scripts from the HTML webpages. Script filtering is managed inside the profiles as we can see in the following screenshot:

5. **Antivirus scanning**: Its control is based on the same concepts we have explained in the dedicated paragraph, previously in this chapter.

 To have a deep dive about the UTM features of a FortiGate please refer to the following document: *FortiOS Handbook Unified Threat Management for FortiOS 5.0* at `http://docs.fortinet.com/fgt/handbook/50/fortigate-utm-50.pdf`.

Client reputation

Client reputation is a tool to track client behaviors and actions that could increase our exposure to attacks. This feature does not give a mechanism to stop the dangerous activities, but highlights them by enabling the administrator to apply security policies and controls as needed. Client reputation is enabled by navigating to the **Security Profiles | Client Reputation | Threat Level Definition** menu shown in the following screenshot:

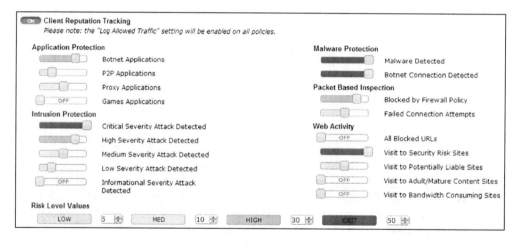

The controls that can be enabled include:

- Bad connection attempts, typical of BOT (an automated or semi-automated tool) activity
- Packets that are blocked by deny-security policies
- Intrusion protection, malware protection, application protection, and web filtering events
- Activities that include visiting websites in risky categories and consuming a high level of bandwidth

Traffic shaping

Inside a security policy we are able to assign a **Traffic Shaping** configuration. The parameters include minimum as well as maximum levels of bandwidth to be able to guarantee **QOS (Quality of Service)**. Traffic shaping is configured by navigating to the **Firewall Objects | Traffic Shaper** pane (shown in the following screenshot):

Name	Test Traffic Shape	
Apply Shaper	● Per Policy ○ For All Policies Using This Shaper	
☑ Maximum Bandwidth	0	(1-2097000 KBps)
☑ Guaranteed Bandwidth	0	(1-2097000 KBps)
Traffic Priority	High ▼	

There are three shaping options available, which are as follows:

- **Shared policy shaping**: Bandwidth management by security policies
- **Per-IP shaping**: Bandwidth management by user IP addresses
- **Application control shaping**: Bandwidth management by application

More information is available in the document *Traffic Shaping for FortiOS 5.0*, available at `http://bit.ly/1dlFHmA`.

Security policies

Security policies will define which session matches with one or more rules in a set and the actions the FortiGate unit will perform. The list of elements that a FortiGate will check includes:

- Source Interface/Zone
- Source Address
- Destination Interface/Zone
- Destination Address
- Schedule and time of the session's initiation
- Service and the packet's port numbers
- UTM profiles

Based on the policies, a packet can be **accepted** or **denied**. Security policies are managed by navigating to the **Policy | Policy | Policy** menu. In the following screenshot we can see the screen used to edit a security policy:

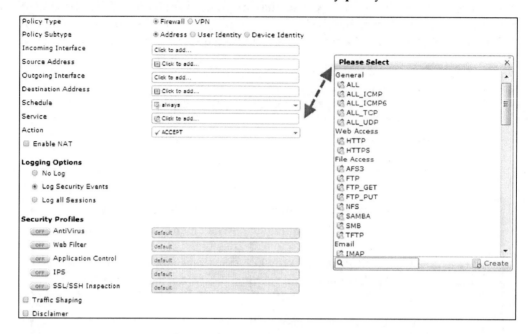

After we have defined a firewall policy, it will look like the following screenshot. Inside a single policy firewall, the controls will be applied in the order we have selected. The firewall policies are evaluated in order from top to bottom. The first rule to match a packet will perform the action specified by the matched rule.

Seq.#	From	To	Source	Destination	Schedule	Service	Auth	Action
1	any	any	all	SSLVPN_TUNNEL_ADDR1	always	ALL		✓ Accept
2	any	any	any	any	always	ALL		⊘ Deny

More information about security policies and the features of the FortiGate firewall is available in the FortiOS Handbook *Firewall for FortiOS 5.0* (at `http://docs.fortinet.com/fgt/handbook/50/fortigate-firewall-50.pdf`).

FortiClient

FortiClient is an endpoint management software available in the following two versions:

- **Standalone client**: This is a free client that offers protection from viruses, malware and adware, and comes with parental control and VPN connection support

- **Managed client**: It is a client which requires a license and it adds to the previously mentioned features, a series of tools for central management, an application firewall, and a vulnerability scan feature

Up to ten managed clients are available for free, then the number of clients that we are able to license depends on the type of FortiGate unit we are using. The client software is available for Microsoft Windows (Windows 8, Windows 7, Windows Vista, and Windows XP) and for Mac OS X (10.8, 10.7, and 10.6). On the *FortiClient* page (http://www.forticlient.com/) we also have apps for iOS (for iOS 5.1 or higher) and Android (Android 4.0 or higher). FortiClient can also be downloaded from the *Fortinet Customer Service & Support* page (https://support.fortinet. com/). In FortiOS v 5.0 Patch Release 1 or later, FortiClient installation files are available for download inside the FortiGate dashboard menu. By navigating to **Selecting System | Dashboard | Status | License**, we can select the Windows or Mac OS version as shown in the following screenshot:

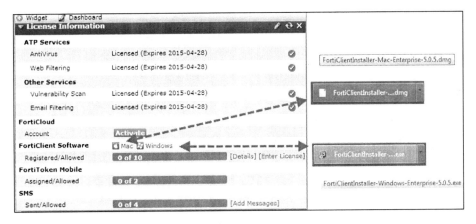

Installation of the FortiClient software can be done manually or by using automated methods such as Microsoft System Center or via the Active Directory policies.

FortiClient management

The first step required is to enable one or more interfaces on the FortiGate unit for **Device Management**. The option is contained in the interface configuration (navigate to the **System | Network | Interfaces** pane) as we can see in the following screenshot:

In the previously mentioned configuration page, we have an option (**Security Mode**) that adds a control on the endpoints. We are able to make an up-to-date installation of the FortiClient software, mandatory on the endpoint. Non-compliant devices will be restricted to a captive portal that provides a downloadable installer of the FortiClient. The captive portal is customizable to be tailored for our company's needs. By navigating to the **Policy | Policy | Policy** menu, we can create a **Device Identity** policy to manage non-compliant devices and unknown devices (see the configuration page in the following screenshot).

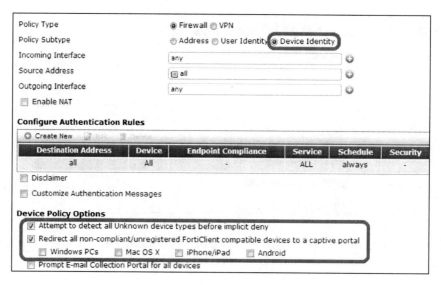

We need to create one or more **client endpoint profiles** by navigating to the **User & Device | Device | Endpoint Profile** menu. A profile enables the management of all the client features, including antivirus, firewall, and VPN. The following screenshot shows the configuration screen for an endpoint profile:

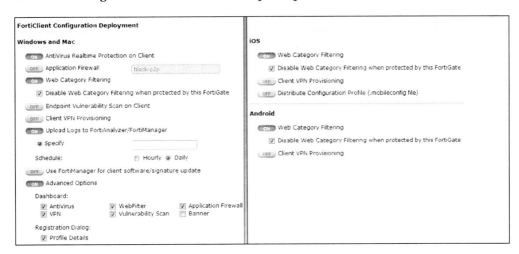

Bring Your Own Device (BYOD)

The policies and configurations we have explained for the FortiClient software can be seen as a part of a larger management scope, dedicated to controls on personal mobile devices connected to our network. The full list of controls includes:

- Identifying and monitoring the devices
- Using the MAC address to control access
- Creating policies based on device type
- Enforcing endpoint control using the FortiClient software

We have already seen the option (inside the interface configuration) to enable device monitoring. The resulting data is included in the **Device definition** menu under the **Device** tab in the **User & Device** option. In the following screenshot, we have an Android tablet and a Windows laptop connected to our FortiGate unit:

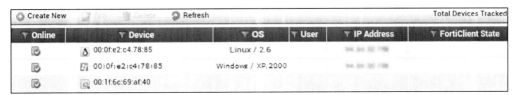

MAC filtering is useful to limit access to our Wi-Fi network. If we enable a DHCP server on our interface, the default value is to assign an IP address to any MAC. We are able to apply a stricter control changing the option for **Unknown MAC Addresses** to **Block** as shown in the following screenshot:

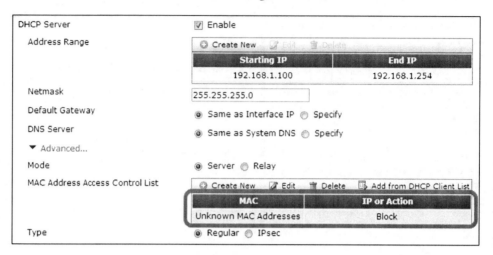

For more information about the FortiClient software a good starting point is the *FortiClient Administration Guide* (the last release is the *v5.0 Patch Release 5* available at
`http://docs.fortinet.com/fclient/forticlient-admin-505.pdf`). For BYOD and client reputation refer to the *FortiOS Handbook Devices and Client Reputation for FortiOS 5.0* (at `http://docs.forticare.com/fgt/handbook/50/fortigate-devices-client-reputation-50.pdf`).

Summary

During this chapter we have introduced the firewall features of FortiGate and the tools dedicated to device management. UTM and the related security and profiles have been presented, and we have seen also a short explanation of the FortiClient software, that adds many administrative mechanisms for endpoint control. In the next chapter we will talk about expanding our network in a secure manner using VPNs and tunnelling.

3
VPNs and Tunneling

A **Virtual Private Network (VPN)** enables computers connected via an insecure network (for example, the Internet) to establish secure connections to work on a private network using a virtual point-to-point connection that prevents eavesdropping by external parties. VPN technologies guarantee security and privacy on the communication using various techniques of authentication and encryption. As soon as the computer or user is connected through a virtual channel, they can benefit from the additional reliability of the internal network, including network policies and security controls dedicated to the endpoints. The VPN client has a level of access to data that is usually reserved for a LAN client. VPN technologies are also widely used for another purpose: to secure connection between multiple offices in different geographical locations. In such a scenario we are using a low cost data network (public or shared), without compromising the trustworthiness of the information. There are two kinds of VPNs based on Fortinet solutions that we are able to use. The first type (client to site) is usually dedicated to end users and is available using the FortiClient software or through the SSL-VPN (web) Portal. The second type (site to site) uses the VPN capabilities of the FortiGate units to connect two devices across a public network. The latter is the one we use to extend our private network on a multisite scenario.

In this chapter we will cover the following topics:

- SSL VPNs
- IPsec VPNs

> In this chapter, we will not specify the different TCP/IP ports that have to be reachable to allow the various types of connection we are going to use. A complete document **Traffic Types and TCP/UDP Ports used by Fortinet Products** is available on the Fortinet site at `http://kb.fortinet.com/kb/microsites/microsite.do?cmd=displayKC&externalId=10773`

FortiGate VPNs are based on the generation of secure **tunnels** through an insecure network. In tunneling, we have a delivery protocol that encapsulates (encrypts) the real data, that is carried by the payload protocol. Information is visible in clear text only on both ends of the connection (that's why we use a similitude with a tunnel for this type of communication).

SSL VPN

In an SSL VPN, we use a typical mechanism, with the delivery protocol (SSL/TLS) working on a higher level of the TCP/IP stack than the payload protocols (TCP/UDP) as shown in the following diagram:

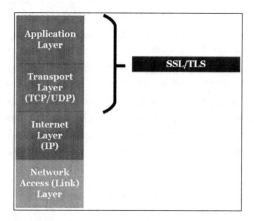

Transport Layer Security (TLS) and the older protocol, **Secure Sockets Layer (SSL)**, are cryptographic protocols based on X.509 digital certificates. For example, every time we access a website that uses HTTPS (such as a secure banking website, for example), we are working over an SSL/TLS secured connection. The process to set up the connection is called "SSL Handshake". It is a client-server process that we are able to divide into five steps:

1. A user (or computer) starts the communication requiring an SSL connection.
2. The server will send its SSL certificate, including the server's public key.

3. The client verifies the certificate and if it is valid, creates, encrypts, and sends back a symmetric session key using the server's public key.

4. The server decrypts the symmetric session key using its private key and sends back an acknowledgement that includes a session key.

5. All subsequent data is now encrypted with the session key.

Talking about the connection from a client, we have two types of SSL VPNs: **Web-Only Mode** and **Tunnel Mode**.

Introduction to SSL VPN portal with web-only mode

Web-only mode enables any authorized user with a supported web browser (the requirements are built-in SSL encryption and Java runtime support) to access, in a secure manner, services such as HTTP/HTTPS, Telnet, FTP, RDP, and SSH.

After the user has established a successful SSL connection with the FortiGate unit, the available services will be shown on a web portal. In a FortiGate unit we have a default web access portal configuration available. A user that opens the SSL VPN portal will see a page as shown in the following screenshot:

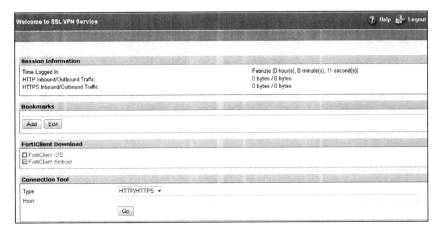

Introduction to SSL VPN portal with tunnel mode

This solution enables the creation of a VPN tunnel by simply logging in to the web SSL VPN portal. The capability of the FortiGate unit to create a tunnel with no software installation required adds flexibility, expanding our scenarios to every system containing a supported browser. The option to download the full client is available to users and makes sense if our configuration is particularly complex (for example, requiring services such as Voice or Video over IP) or diversified across various users. In the following screenshot the portal containing only the tunneling option is shown:

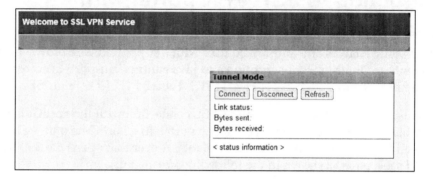

As soon as the client is connected to the HTTPS tunnel, our security configuration may require:

- To encrypt all the traffic (redirecting everything over the HTTPS tunnel)
- To leave all the network packets flow unencrypted from the client to the Internet connection if they are not directed to our internal network (split tunnel option)

There are certain requirements to consider when making a choice between full or split tunnel configurations. The configuration without split tunnel is more secure. However, the VPN connected client is configured with the same parameters required by a device in the internal network (including the configuration required to browse the Internet). All the data traffic will traverse the firewall and this solution may, in addition, create delays and bottlenecks. Split tunnel is a less stringent choice, but we must consider the risk that the client becomes a point of uncontrolled passage for Internet related risks (because the user is accessing our systems while using public resources from a non-secure workplace). The standard process consists of the following steps:

1. The FortiGate unit authenticates remote users. Local users, local groups, and remote identities authenticated via services such as Radius and Active Directory services are supported.

2. The browser is redirected to the portal page.

3. A verification of the installed VPN client (ActiveX or Java) occurs. The plugin is installed if needed. As an alternative, the SSL VPN tunnel can also be initiated from a standalone app.

4. The client receives a virtual network address from a pool or range of IPs we have dedicated to the VPN connected devices and starts to use it as its source address.

Configuring the SSL VPN portal

To enable SSL VPN portal operations, it is required that we act on different services of our FortiGate unit. We need to configure the following items.

SSL VPN settings:

- SSL VPN portal
- Users and groups
- Policy

Configuring the SSL VPN settings

First step is the configuration of the base parameters in the **Config** menu (navigate to **VPN | SSL | Config**). We can see the available options in the following screenshot, including **Addresses** that will be dedicated to the SSL VPN clients (using tunnel mode), the type of SSL server certificate (**Server Certificate**) we will use, **Idle Timeout**, and the **Login port** options:

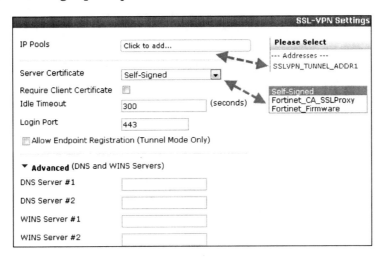

We can configure a subnet or a range of addresses to use as an IP Pool. Both the aforementioned addresses are managed using the **Address** menu (navigate to **Firewall Objects | Address | Address**) as we have seen in the section *Addresses* in *Chapter 2, Filters, Policies, and Endpoint Security*.

Configuring the SSL VPN portal

The **Portal** menu (navigate to **VPN | SSL | Portal**) is dedicated to the creation of different views when a user logs into the VPN portal. As we mentioned in the previous section, there are three default configurations available for the portal (full-access, tunnel-access, and web-access), but we are able to create additional portal settings to fit our company's requirements. We can build a tailored portal using two basic modes, Tunnel Mode and Web Mode. To simplify the explanation, we can divide the screen into four zones as shown in the following screenshot:

The four zones are explained in the following list:

- At the top we have parameters related to the appearance of the portal, including a custom welcome message, the color scheme applied to the page, and the layout (one or two columns).

- The second zone is dedicated to the tunnel mode, and requires one or more groups of IP addresses that will be deployed to the connected clients as virtual network addresses. The configuration provides also the choice to activate split tunneling.

- The third zone is dedicated to web mode. Here we can publish or hide the applications, include tools to make them available to the user, and add bookmarks. Bookmarks are pre-configured connections to internal network resources, including internal server addresses, listening ports, and (if required) security information such as user and password. We can see the options related to the bookmarks in the following screenshot:

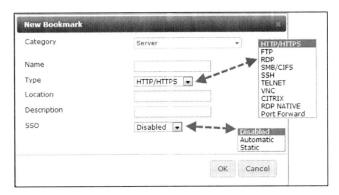

- The last zone includes the options related to the FortiClient app download and a button to have a preview of the portal we are working on.

Configuring users and groups for the SSL VPN portal

If we have not yet configured users or groups in the FortiGate unit (or if we need to create a few dedicated for SSL VPNs) we can use the two menus: **User Definition** (navigate to **User & Devices | User | User Definition**) and **User Group** (navigate to **User & Devices | User | User Group**).

Configuring a policy for the SSL VPN portal

We need a last configuration to define users and groups enabled to see the SSL VPN portals we have configured in the previous steps. The aforementioned administrative task is performed in the **Policy** menu (navigate to **Policy | Policy | Policy**). As shown in the following screenshot, the first step is to define an SSL VPN policy including source and destination of our rule:

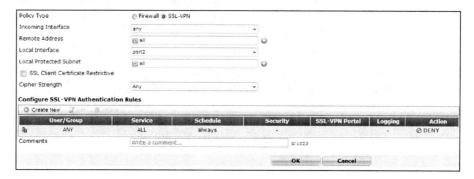

The second required step is to create a new authentication rule inside the SSL VPN policy. The aforementioned rule will define the portal that users will be able to access and a schedule that will allow access only on a certain time frame. An authentication rule configuration screen is shown in the following screenshot:

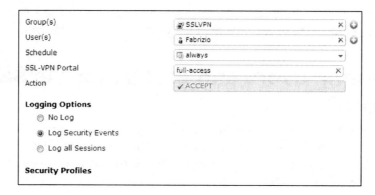

FortiGate IPsec VPN

In the section where we introduced the SSL VPN, we said that looking at the TCP/IP protocol stack, usually the delivery protocol is located on a higher level than the payload protocol. This statement is not valid for the next type of VPN, which will be discussed. An IPsec VPN secures each IP (Internet Protocol) packet with authentication and encryption. IPsec uses two different protocols: **AH** and **ESP**, to provide authentication, integrity, and confidentiality of the communication. Basic operations related to IPsec include:

- **Transport mode**: Only the payload of the IP datagram is handled by IPsec, which inserts the header between the IP header and the upper levels.

- **Tunnel mode**: This is used to protect the entire IP datagram. This is the base of an IPsec VPN that creates a "Layer 3 tunnel". The original packet is encapsulated in a new IP packet (the header of the new packet is IPsec).

In the following diagram we have a schema that shows an original packet compared with the packets resulting using the two IPsec modes:

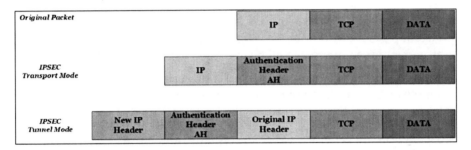

As we stated earlier, a VPN tunnel can be built between two FortiGate devices (or between a FortiGate unit and a client) to create a point-to-point connection, which uses the Internet as its data communication channel. In the following sections we will see IPsec VPN configurations, with an emphasis on the ones involving two or more FortiGate units.

Configuring an IPsec VPN

FortiGate has a dedicated interface for VPN configuration, the **Auto Key (IKE)** menu (navigate to **VPN | IPSEC | Auto Key (IKE)**). Here we are able to manage the two phases of IPsec tunneling:

- **Phase 1 parameters**: These are required to identify the remote peer and include information required to authenticate the other endpoint of the VPN.

- **Phase 2 parameters**: As soon as phase 1 is correctly finished, phase 2 defines the encryption algorithm that will be used during a session.

 Internet Key Exchange (IKE) is the protocol used to set up a security association (shared security attributes like encryption key, algorithm, and mode) in an IPsec protocol.

In the following screenshot we are able to see the **Auto Key (IKE)** menu. To define configuration for the aforementioned phases we will use the **Create Phase 1** and **Create Phase 2** buttons.

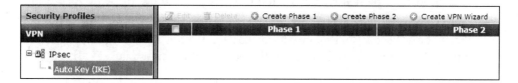

In a FortiGate unit we have two types of VPN available: policy-based or route-based:

- A route-based VPN (also known as an interface-based VPN) creates a virtual IPsec network interface. All the network traffic passing through the aforementioned interface will be managed using the VPN rules.
- A policy-based VPN is implemented configuring a security policy (defining source and destination) with an action of IPsec and then selecting the VPN tunnel we want to use to manage the traffic included in the rule.

Route-based VPNs are generally easier to configure and more flexible in their application. However, certain scenarios may require policy-based VPNs. To explain the basic configuration steps, we will see the first type of IPsec VPN involving two devices that is called **Gateway-to-Gateway**.

Designing a Gateway-to-Gateway VPN

The aforementioned solution requires at least two FortiGate units to create an encrypted and secured communication channel between two private networks based on a VPN tunnel.

 A VPN gateway is a FortiGate unit located at one end of a tunnel that receives packets incoming from the VPN connection and sends them to the local network after decryption. It is also responsible to encrypt data sent to the device on the other end of the secure connection.

In the following schema we are able to see a basic design for our Gateway-to-Gateway configuration:

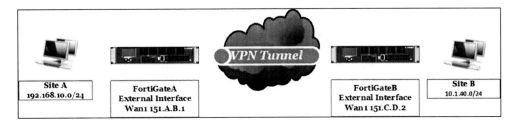

The first step will be defining a new phase 1 by navigating to the **VPN | IPSEC | Auto Key (IKE)** menu. On the FortiGateA unit we will configure the parameters shown in the following screenshot (only the top part of the menu is shown):

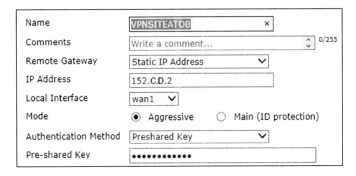

We will use **Name** that reflects the use of the VPN tunnel that we are going to configure. Depending on our scenario, **Remote Gateway** can be defined using a static IP address, a dynamic DNS (DDNS) name, or a dialup user, explained as follows:

- Static IP is usually associated with remote devices having a dedicated Internet connection.

- DDNS is used to associate a static configuration to a device that does not have a static public IP. Each time a device receives a new address on the public network, it will contact the DNS server and update the IP address associated with his host name. This allows the use of the host name registered in the DDNS as a parameter inside a configuration without having to worry when the IP changes.

- Dialup user is usually associated with VPN connections that are initiated from the other end of the VPN tunnel, for example, from a FortiClient.

Local Interface is the interface used for the IPsec tunnel traffic. **Mode** is a parameter required only if we are going to use IKE version 1. IKE sends a proposal at the beginning of a session to define the **security association (SA)**. Usually the process requires multiple (encrypted) information exchange. This standard behavior is defined in **Main** mode. The **Aggressive** mode decreases the number of packets dedicated to IKE SA negotiation to three with authentication information not encrypted. **Authentication Method** is used to define how the FortiGate unit can authenticate itself and the remote FortiGate unit. Available options are **Preshared Key** or **RSA Signature (certificate)**.

The remaining parameters in the menu are related to **Peer Options** (authentication requirements for the other endpoint of our VPN) and to customize IKE parameters (an action that we will perform only if required by our scenario).

The second step required is the configuration of a new phase 2 to define the encryption and authentication algorithms. If we are fine with the default parameters, the only information required is the **Name** that will be associated with this phase 2 and **Phase 1** we want to use for it as we can see in the following screenshot:

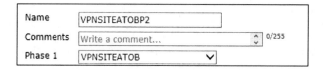

 The tunnel interface name will be defined from the name used in phase 1.

Navigating the **System | Network | Interface** menu, we will see the tunnel in the list of available interfaces (see the following screenshot):

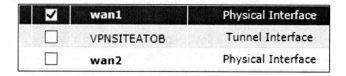

Phase 1 and phase 2 configuration are required also on the second unit (FortiGateB). Two steps are still required: configuring a security policy that will allow the traffic to flow from one network to the other and adding a route to make the traffic flow through the VPN tunnel. Navigate to the **Policy | Policy | Policy** menu, we will add an accept policy for traffic from Site A to Site B like the one shown in the following screenshot:

Seq.#	▼ Source	▼ Destination	▼ Schedule	▼ Service	▼ Authentication	▼ Action
▼ internal - VPNSITEATOB (1 - 1)						
1	🖭 IP_192.168.10.0/24	🖭 IP_10.1.40.0/24	🕒 always	🗔 ALL		✓ Accept

To complete the configuration we will add a static route so that all the traffic to the remote network will pass through the virtual VPN interface as shown in the following screenshot:

We will execute similar operations on the other FortiGate unit.

Hub-and-Spoke VPN

A scenario that extends what we have seen up to this point is the one that uses a central FortiGate unit (**Hub**) to act as a pivot to the connection of a series of remote networks, each one placed behind a FortiGate peer (**Spokes**). A simple schema will look like the one shown in the following diagram:

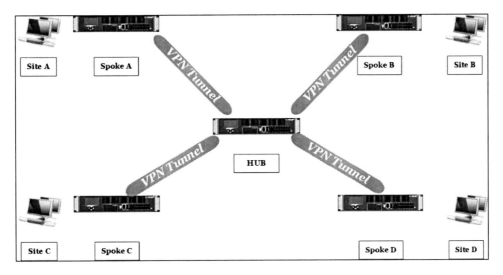

The configuration steps do not differ much from those we have already seen for the spokes. As shown in the diagram, all the tunnels are terminated on the hub, requiring configuration of a VPN from every single spoke to the hub. On the hub some additional configurations are required:

- It is necessary to have a static public IP address on the hub, while spokes can still use DDNS and dialup
- We will have to configure a VPN on the hub for every single spoke

Depending on the type of VPN we have configured in the previous steps, we will have two different procedures to enable the hub-and-spoke VPN.

For a policy-based VPN:

- Two security policies are required (type VPN and subtype IPsec) for each spoke (one policy for every direction)
- The hub is configured as a VPN concentrator

A concentrator allows traffic between the networks connected to the various spokes passing traffic from one tunnel to another. On the hub, from the CLI, we can use the `config VPN ipsec concentrator` command that is structured as we can see in the following schema:

- `config vpn ipsec concentrator`
    - `edit <concentrator_name>` (Enter a name for the concentrator)
    - `set member <member_name> <member_name>` (Enter the names of up to three VPN tunnels to add to the concentrator. Separate the tunnel names with spaces)

To enable route-based VPN we are required to configure security policies (type firewall and subtype address). There are three different ways to configure this kind of VPN:

- Gather all the IPsec interfaces into a zone and enable intra-zone traffic as we can see in the following screenshot:

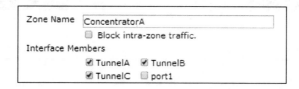

Note that UTM features will not be available with this configuration.

- Gather all IPsec interfaces into a zone and create a single zone-to-zone security policy. The first step will be similar to the one seen in the previous screenshot, but we will leave the **Block intra-zone traffic** flag selected. Then we will configure a security policy to allow traffic to and from the zone, as shown in the following screenshot:

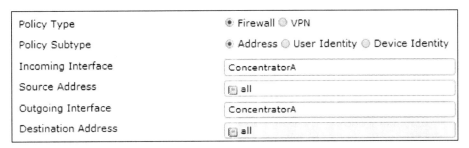

This is a configuration similar to the previous one, but in this situation we are able to apply UTM controls.

- Create a security policy for each pair of spokes that are allowed to communicate with each other. For example, let's say that we have **TunnelA** connecting the hub to **SpokeA** and **TunnelC** connecting the hub to **SpokeC**. The policy will be similar to the one we can see in the following screenshot:

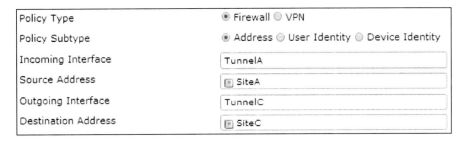

Dialup VPN

VPN configuration, as we can see in the following screenshot, also includes the possibility to accept incoming dialup connections as remote endpoints of our tunnel:

This allows VPN clients, behind a NAT or with dynamic IP addresses, to connect to the public IP of the hub firewall. The FortiGate unit configured to act as a dialup client will require a VPN configuration like the ones we have already seen, pointing to a static public IP. We will configure security policies and routes as we would do for a standard tunnel. Since the client usually connects from a dynamic IP address, it is the responsibility of the client to initiate the VPN tunnel to the hub. We can create multiple dialup tunnels on a single interface, but only if we use Xauth and main mode (not aggressive mode). Dialup VPN will require a user or a group for the authentication phase.

FortiClient dialup client

In *Chapter 2, Filters, Policies, and Endpoint Security*, while talking about FortiClient, we said that the software includes support for VPN connections. This is an option that extends the capability to create a private connection with our corporate network to the mobile users (including the ones that are working using a smartphone or a tablet). The IP address of the mobile device could be dynamic or static, with or without an active NAT translation. If a NAT is in-place, **NAT traversal (NAT-T)** compatibility is required, to allow encrypted packets to flow from the device to the FortiGate unit. The FortiClient download portal and the VPN setting distribution require TCP ports 8009 and 8900, respectively, to be reachable from the FortiClient to the FortiGate unit. VPN setting distribution allows the automatic configuration of the FortiClient for the VPN usage. The only parameter the user has to know is the public IP of the FortiGate tunnel interface. The client will then connect to the appliance and, after authentication, will download VPN parameters (including phase 1 and phase 2 settings) directly from the FortiGate unit. To enable dialup from the FortiClient, the easiest way is to use **Create VPN Wizard**, which is available by navigating to the **VPN | IPSEC | Auto Key (IKE)** menu. The first step will require the type of client that will connect through the dialup, as shown in the following screenshot:

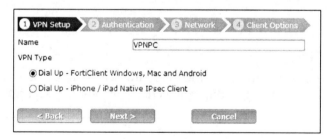

The second step requires the pre-shared key for the connection and the user group to enable the dialup VPN. Next step contains information about the outgoing interface and two important settings, highlighted in the following screenshot:

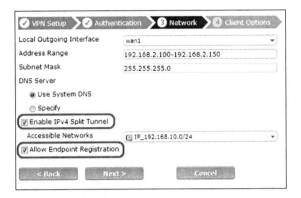

Enable IPv4 Split Tunnel is used to enable split tunneling, that will work as we have seen earlier while explaining about SSL VPN. **Allow Endpoint Registration** enables the FortiGate unit to require a registration key from FortiClient before a connection can be established. The last screen of the wizard contains three user options, **Save Password**, **Auto Connect**, and **Always Up (Keep Alive)**. The latter option will keep the client connected also during an inactive period. As soon as the client starts a VPN connection, authentication parameters will be required, as we can see in the following screenshot:

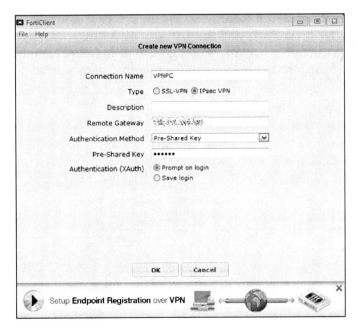

L2TP VPN

FortiGate units include the capability to accept L2TP VPN connections from a Windows client using the built-in software, without the need to install FortiClient. Starting with Windows 2000, the operating system has a built-in L2TP client. An L2TP packet consists of a datagram with two additional headers: one UDP and one L2TP, as shown in the following diagram:

L2TP Packet	IP Header	UDP Header	L2TP Header	PPP Header	DATA

Using UDP, L2TP is not encrypted and depends on IPsec to secure packets. The resulting encapsulation is the one we can see in the following diagram:

L2TP Packet With IPSEC	IP Header	IPSEC ESP Header	UDP Header	L2TP Header	PPP Header	DATA	IPSEC ESP Trailer	IP Auth Trailer

Authentication for L2TP VPN in a FortiGate unit is based on users and groups. In a scenario like this, with Microsoft clients connecting, it could be required not to use local accounts, but to forward authentication requests to an external trusted authority, such as a Windows Directory Server, using LDAP or Radius. External authentication providers are configured inside the **Authentication** menu (navigate to **User & Device | Authentication**). LDAP Server is a solution that makes sense if the FortiGate unit is able to connect directly to an **AD DS (Active Directory Domain Services)** server. The required parameters are the server IP address (**Server Name/ IP**), listening port (**Server Port**), and the distinguished name (**Distinguished Name**) on the directory structure where users and groups used for VPN authentication are stored. The following screenshot displays the required parameters:

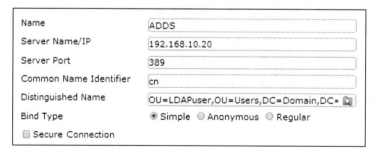

Remote Authentication Dial in User Service (RADIUS) enables authentication with a client-server schema in which the FortiGate unit will receive authentication requests from the VPN user and forwards them to a radius server (usually a Microsoft server that is joined to our domain) for approval. The main advantage of this protocol is the fact that a direct connection to an AD DS server is no longer required, enhancing the security of our network. Radius can be configured by navigating to the **User & Device | Authentication** menu. The administrative panel for radius is shown in the following screenshot:

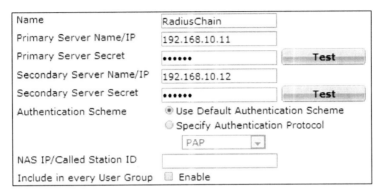

The only required parameters are the IP address of the radius server and a shared secret phrase that will allow communication from the appliance to the server. As soon as the users and groups are defined, we have to configure a local address range to reserve for remote L2TP clients. The aforementioned administrative task requires the use of the `config vpn l2tp` command in the CLI. The command has the following structure:

- `config vpn l2tp`
  - `set eip <address_ipv4>` (ending IP address of the address range)
  - `set sip <address_ipv4>` (starting IP address of the address range)
  - `set status {enable | disable}` (enable or disable L2TP VPN)
  - `set usrgrp <group_name>` (user group for authenticating L2TP clients)

Security policies will require the use of aforementioned address range to identify the L2TP clients. Note that it is also required to configure IPsec for L2TP, performing the same steps we have seen in the previous sections.

Summary

During this chapter we have introduced the VPN features available for a FortiGate unit, including the different options available to extend our network or to enable mobile users for the access to our internal network in a secure manner. Next chapter will be focused on the high availability and load balancing features we are able to deploy when we use one or more FortiGate appliances. We will also introduce the concept of **VDOM (Virtual Domain)**.

4

High Availability

The typical role of a FortiGate unit, a gateway to external networks and to the Internet, requires safeguards to prevent the following two problems:

- Failure of a single unit that could bring an interruption of network services
- Network traffic overloads that could create a bottleneck effect on the network traffic

Both these scenarios would have unacceptable consequences on the reliability and usability of the network. To avoid the problem related to failures, Fortinet proposes four different solutions, which are as follows:

- **FortiGate Cluster Protocol (FGCP)**: This solution enables us to aggregate two or more FortiGate devices into one logical unit (**cluster**). A cluster eliminates the single point of failure and FGCP allows us to configure the cluster units in two different structures: active-passive or active-active. Active-active configuration also relieves network traffic, balancing the load on all the available cluster units and preventing bottlenecks. FGCP is a very robust clustering protocol and is the default protocol when configuring high availability.

- **FortiGate Session Life Support Protocol (FGSP)**: This solution requires an external load balancer. Sessions using IPv4, IPv6, TCP, UDP, ICMP, and NAT are synchronized on the FortiGate units. If one of the FortiGate units fails, a session failover occurs without any data loss. In such a configuration, balancing and failover are performed by the external device while maintenance of the session table on all units is performed by FGSP.

- **Virtual Router Redundancy Protocol (VRRP)**: VRPP is an open standard, described in RFC5798, which is designed to bring resiliency and redundancy to layer 3 routers and switches. FortiGate can be integrated into a VRRP group with any third-party devices. VRRP supports configurations with multiple FortiGate units (in a master-backup couple) or configurations with a third-party router (usually the master in this scenario is the FortiGate unit). In the event of a failover, only the configuration with two FortiGate units keeps UTM capabilities.

- **Fortinet Redundant UTM Protocol (FRUP)**: In *Chapter 1*, *First Steps* we talked about software switches to group independent interfaces into a single logical interface that has a unique IP address. In FortiOS 5.0, for FortiGate models that have internal hardware switches, we can group interfaces in the hardware switch into virtual hardware switches. The FortiGate units will have a double connection towards one another, one active and one passive. The configuration will be inverted on the two units. Using virtual MACs and IPs FRUP will support failover.

> For a practical example of a FRUP configuration refer to the **Fortinet Redundant UTM Protocol (FRUP)** at `http://docs.fortinet.com/fgt/cookbook/supplement/FRUP.pdf`.

Link aggregation

The previously mentioned solutions mitigate the risk related to having a FortiGate unit as a single point of failure. However, we need to implement a configuration to prevent a single port (on the appliance or on the network switch) from becoming critical, in case of a failure. We will use **link aggregation** (typically referred to as NIC teaming, teaming, EtherChannel or Link Aggregation Group) to combine multiple network connections and provide redundancy in case one of the links fails. We can use **802.3ad** link aggregation to combine two or more interfaces into a single logical aggregated link. We will also see how to use an automation protocol for operations related to link aggregation, the **Link Aggregation Control Protocol (LACP)**. LACP manages tasks related to the distribution of traffic among the physical interfaces we have aggregated. Without LACP, we should manually set additional parameters for link aggregation. 802.3ad aggregation is managed by navigating to the **System | Network | Interface** menu. In the following screenshot we have an example configuration of a new logical aggregated link called `Aggregate1` that includes **port3** and **port4** on our FortiGate unit. The remaining parameters are the same as those we have already seen for a physical interface.

> If LACP is not in use, we need to run a command in the CLI to get the 802.3ad configured and working correctly. Many switches will not forward traffic correctly unless the following code is configured in the FortiGate unit:
>
>
>
> ```
> edit "Interface Name"
> set lacp-mode static
> next
> ```
>
> This code sets the aggregate as a static non LACP and makes it work with any switch.

Virtual MAC addresses

As we know, each network interface has a unique **MAC** address (**Media Access Control**, a unique identifier used to communicate on the physical network segment). The devices and computers connected to our network match every IP address to a MAC address and this information is saved in the ARP cache. The data in the ARP cache is used until their expiration time is reached. So if a cluster should be presented with the MAC addresses of the physical adapters on the different FortiGate units, this would make high reliability impossible because network connected devices would keep searching the MAC address of a failed FortiGate unit until the ARP cache expiration. The solution used for the FGCP protocol, for example, is to assign a **virtual** MAC address for every single network interface on the primary unit in the cluster. If a failure occurs on the unit, there will be no change in the MAC associated with the highly available IP address. To update the layer 2 switches that are directly connected with the FortiGate units, in case of a failover or when a failback happens, the primary unit uses so-called **Gratuitous ARP (GARP)** packets. This type of network packet is used to force an update in the ARP cache of the switches that are attached to the unit's interfaces. It is not possible (or advisable) to disable GARP packets.

The configuration related to GARP is based on the `config system ha` command in the CLI. The command has the following structure:

- `config system ha`

  ○ `set arps <number>`: This limits the number of GARP packets sent

  ○ `set arps-interval <seconds, value range 1-20>`: It configures the time between ARP packets

FortiGate Cluster Protocol

As we have said, **FortiGate Cluster Protocol (FCGP)** provides failover protection (the clustered firewall services are available even after a failure on the primary unit). To explain the FGCP protocol, we can start from a practical example, showing the steps required to configure two FortiGate units (`FortiGate_Master` and `FortiGate_Slave`) in a cluster to connect two networks linked to the interfaces `wan1` and `wan2` with high availability (HA). The schema of this scenario is the one we can see in the following diagram:

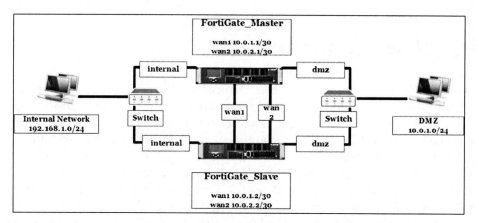

As shown in the previous image, four network interfaces are required for each firewall. At least one port on every FortiGate must be dedicated to the connection to the two networks. The third and fourth network interfaces are dedicated to the connection between the two FortiGate units and are used for **heartbeat** (exchange of communication and synchronization of the information that allows a cluster to form).

 Configuring the cluster with a single cable for the connection between the units is possible, but it is not recommended if we are using more than two units in the cluster.

If a single cable per unit is going from `FortiGate_Master` and `FortiGate_Slave` to one of the networks, they have to be connected to the same switch. As we said in the previous paragraph, link aggregation based on 802.3ad protocol is available to add redundancy, with multiple switches connected to a cluster interface. We will start from the primary FortiGate unit, `FortiGate_Master`, in our schema. Our first step will be assigning an IP address to `wan1` and `wan2` as we can see in the following screenshot (an internal port will be used to manage the single units).

wan1	Physical Interface	10.0.1.1 / 255.255.255.252	PING
wan2	Physical Interface	10.0.2.1 / 255.255.255.252	PING
internal	Physical Interface	192.168.1.99 / 255.255.255.0	HTTP,HTTPS,PING,SSH,CAPWAP,FMG-Access

Then we will manage the high availability configuration by navigating to the **System | Config | HA** menu, shown in the following screenshot:

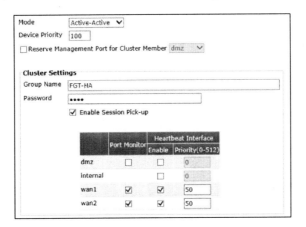

We are able to activate HA with an **Active-Passive mode** or add load balancing using the **Active-Active mode**. As soon as we select a cluster mode, an additional **Reserve Management Port for Cluster Member** option will be available. The idea is to have a non-synchronized interface on every unit, giving a different IP address to each one. This feature is important for the management of **virtual clusters** (we will talk about them later in this chapter). In our scenario we will use an internal port for management. The **Device Priority** parameter is used if we want to manually select the unit in the cluster that will act as the master. The default behavior is to configure the cluster unit with the highest serial number to be the primary unit. If we have two or more devices with a different device priority, the primary unit will always be the one with the highest priority, disregarding the previously mentioned serial number.

Additional selection parameters for a primary unit are the presence of disconnected monitored interfaces and the "age" of the unit.

 Additional details regarding the mentioned parameters used in the selection of the primary unit are available in the *FortiOS Handbook - High Availability for FortiOS 5.0* at http://docs.fortinet.com/fgt/ handbook/50/fortigate-ha-50.pdf.

In the test configuration discussed in this paragraph, we have changed the default value for priority (100) to be equal to 80 on the slave. **Group Name** is required to create a cluster and must be the same on all units of the cluster. As soon as the cluster configuration is synchronized, we are able to perform administrative operations such as the change of the cluster group name and we will have the new configuration updated automatically on all the cluster units. The **Password** parameter is important to control the units that are able to join our cluster (the password must be the same in all the cluster units). The **Enable Session Pick-up** flag is used to activate the failover for TCP, IPSEC, UDP, and ICMP sessions during a failover. If we enable **Port Monitor** on the clustered interfaces, it will activate a failover as soon as an interface is not working properly. In our scenario we will start with an **Active-Active** mode cluster. The HA screen will change, showing a graphical representation of the first node of our cluster like the one in the following screenshot:

Now we have to repeat the configuration steps on the FortiGate_Slave unit. The interface wan1 will have an IP address equal to 10.0.1.2/30 and interface wan2 will have an IP address equal to 10.0.2.2/30. I suggest using small subnets to configure intra-cluster links and to assign them to subnets that are not used for other corporate networks. This makes sense, especially if we are going to distribute connected networks inside a dynamic routing protocol (see *Chapter 1, Introducing OSPF*). The HA parameters will be the ones shown in the following screenshot:

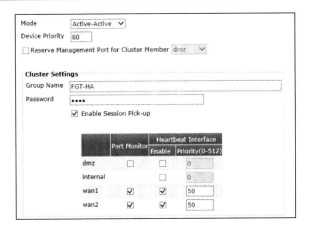

After a short time to synchronize the configurations, `FortiGate_Master` will take the master role and `FortiGate_Slave` will be identified as the slave (the HA configuration screen will be similar to the one in the following screenshot).

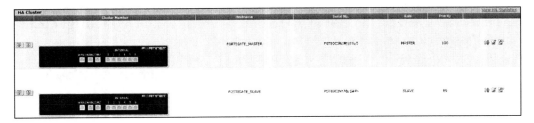

Active-Passive and Active-Active Clusters

An Active-Passive HA cluster is made up of a primary node that answers all the communication requests by one or more **standby** (**subordinate**) units. The subordinate unit will continuously synchronize its configuration with the primary unit. As soon as the master unit is unreachable, one of the subordinate units, that are constantly monitoring the master unit, will take its place in a transparent manner. An Active-Active HA cluster grants the options for failure recovery that we have in an Active-Passive cluster and, in addition, it balances the UTM workload among all the units in the cluster. All the network traffic that is not related to UTM processes is not balanced, and is managed by the primary unit (like in Active-Passive mode). To also load balance all the TCP sessions we can use a CLI command `load-balance-all`. To load balance all the UDP sessions, there is a similar command in the CLI, `load-balance-udp`.

Both the features are disabled by default because the increased overhead associated with full TCP and UDP load balancing is usually something that makes this type of configuration non-recommendable.

[

ICMP, multicast, and broadcast sessions are never load balanced and are always processed by the primary unit.
]

FortiGate Session Life Support Protocol

FortiGate Session Life Support Protocol (FGSP) is used for traffic redundancy if a load balancer is already present in our network. Load balancing and session failover is done by the external balancer while two FortiGate units are integrated with it, to keep session synchronization (in a session table). TCP sessions (by default) and connectionless protocols like UDP and ICMP sessions (with an additional configuration) are able to failover from a unit to the other one with no data loss. Depending on the configuration of the balancer, all the network packets are sent to the primary unit and are directed to the secondary unit in case of a failure (like in the Active-Passive clusters) or the workload is balanced on both units (like in the Active-Active clusters). The configuration of the cluster units is not synchronized by default (this behavior can be modified). A basic schema of an FGSP cluster is shown as follows:

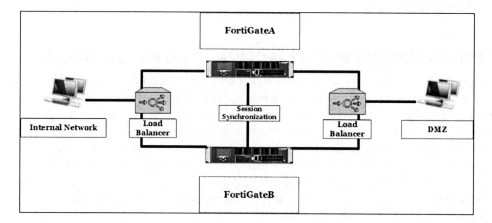

The session synchronization link may include more than one interface, but only a single link is accepted in every configuration. It is required to have a direct connection between the cluster units, with no switch in the middle.

FGSP is configured using the CLI `system session-sync` command. It is possible to pair every FGSP configuration with a filter, used to limit session synchronization only to certain types of connection (for example TCP / HTTP) or to certain source / destination IP addresses. If we have an existing HA configuration, we have to remove it because HA and FGSP are not supported together on the same unit. The system `session-sync` command has the following structure:

- `config system session-sync`
- `edit <sync_id>`: Enter the unique ID number for the session synchronization configuration to edit (any number between 1 and 200).

 It is not necessary to have the same ID number on both the cluster units.

- `set peerip <peer_ipv4>`: Enter the IP address of the interface on the peer unit that is used for the session synchronization link.
- `config filter`: Add a filter to FGSP.
    - `set dstaddr <dst_ip_ipv4> <dst_mask_ipv4>`: Enter the destination IP address of the sessions to synchronize.
    - `set dstintf <interface_name>`: Enter the name of a FortiGate interface. Only sessions destined for this interface are synchronized.
    - `set service <string>`: Only sessions that use this service are synchronized.
    - `set srcaddr <src_ip_ipv4> <src_mask_ipv4>`: Enter the source IP address of the sessions to synchronize.
    - `set srcintf <interface_name>`: Enter the name of a FortiGate interface. Only sessions from this interface are synchronized.

To show an FGSP configuration, let's suppose that our two units, FortiGateA and FortiGateB have a synchronization link on port3, with addresses 192.168.100.100/24 and 192.168.100.101/24. On FortiGateA we will insert the following commands:

```
config system session-sync
edit 10
set peerip 192.168.100.101
end
```

On FortiGateB we will insert the following commands:

```
config system session-sync
edit 11
set peerip 192.168.100.100
end
```

Virtual Router Redundancy Protocol

Virtual Router Redundancy Protocol (VRRP) is a protocol to provide device redundancy with a backup router. If the primary (master) router fails, a backup router takes over. The routers are grouped together in a single virtual router with a single IP address. The master router will always process traffic that is addressed to the virtual router address and sends out regular advertisements to the backup router. If the master experiences a failure, the backup router no longer receives advertisements and becomes the primary router. The VRRP protocol is an open standard and is implemented by many router vendors. FortiGate firewalls can be used in a VRRP cluster with other non-Fortinet devices. The configuration requires using the config vrrp command inside the configuration of the interface that connects to the master unit. The structure of this command is as follows:

- config vrrp
    - ◦ edit <VRID_int>: Enter an ID for the virtual router.
    - ◦ set adv-interval <seconds_int>: Define the virtual router advertisement message interval (between 1 and 255 seconds).
    - ◦ set priority <prio_int>: Enter a priority value for this device.

- ◦ `set start-time <seconds_int>`: Define the time (in seconds) that the backup unit (not receiving advertisement messages) will wait before replacing the master.
- ◦ `set status {enable | disable}`: Used to disable or re-enable the FGSP configuration.
- ◦ `set vrdst <ipv4_addr>`: Monitor the route to a destination IP address.
- ◦ `set vrip <ipv4_addr>`: Enter the virtual IP for the virtual router.

In the following table we have a comparison of the high availability options:

	FGCP	FGSP	VRRP	FRUP
Requirements	The FortiGate units must have the same hardware configuration, firmware build, operating mode, and VDOM mode	Both physical FortiGate units and virtual domains are supported. However a large part of the work is delegated to the external load balancer.	Third party products supporting VRRP are accepted as a master or backup in this configuration	Available only on specified FortiGate models (FortiGate 100D units)
Features	Session failover excluding multicast and SSL VPN sessions Configuration synchronization Load balancing	Session synchronization to support external balancer failover and load balancing.	Routing continuity	Supports dual redundant HA links between the units for sharing session and configuration data
Limitations	Hardware and firmware must be identical	SessioWns including UTM controls are not synchronized Configuration is done only using the CLI	No session synchronization	Requires FortiOS 5.0 Requires specific FortiGate-models

Full mesh high availability

Earlier in the chapter we talked about the link aggregation and 802.3ad protocol. As we said, the mentioned solutions expand redundancy and high availability also to the hardware devices connecting the FortiGate units to the rest of the network (usually network switches). The required configuration is called **Full Mesh HA**. The FortiGate cluster will be connected to the network using redundant connections and switches. In the following diagram, we can see a cluster made up of two units (**FortiGateA** and **FortiGateB**) connected with a full mesh to the internal network:

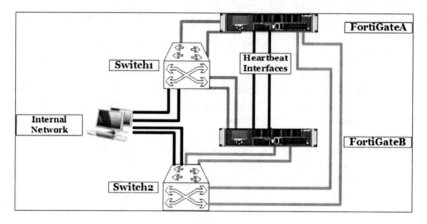

All the connections are redundant, including two interfaces dedicated to the cluster heartbeat. We will use two switches to have the highest level of continuity. Cluster configuration will follow the same steps we have seen when we were talking about FGCP (or FGSP), while the redundant links will be configured using the steps explained earlier in the chapter for the link aggregation.

Introducing virtual domains

Virtual Domains (VDOMs) enable the division of a single FortiGate unit into multiple virtual devices. Each VDOM supports separate settings related to routing, firewalling, and VPN connections. Also if we have decided not to use VDOMs, a virtual domain will always exist: the root VDOM, which is the one we use for the normal management of a FortiGate unit. As soon as we adopt VDOMs, the entire existing configuration will be kept inside the root VDOM. To enable VDOMs we have to use the **Virtual Domain** options, shown in the following screenshot, by navigating to the **System | Dashboard | Status** menu:

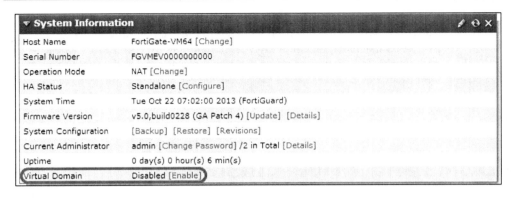

On selecting **Enable** we will be forced to login again to the FortiGate unit. As soon as we open the web-based manager, we will see some changes. The first one is that the left pane is no longer called **System** but is now called **Global**. We will see an additional menu dedicated to **VDOM** configuration. Both changes are shown in the following screenshot:

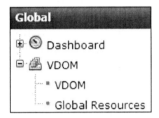

From now on, only accounts included in the `super_admin` profiles can configure global options. An additional menu called **Virtual Domains** will be available in the left pane. The menu contains a list of the enabled VDOMs with the options configured for every single virtual domain. In the following screenshot we have a capture of the submenu dedicated to the root domain:

The concept of VDOM has been included in this chapter only for its impact on the management of high availability (as we will see in the next paragraph). To know more about this topic, please refer to the following document: *FortiOS Handbook Virtual Domains for FortiOS 5.0* at `http://docs.fortinet.com/fgt/handbook/50/fortigate-vdoms-50.pdf`.

VDOMs and virtual clustering

Virtual clustering supports a maximum of two FortiGate units in an FGCP cluster, with multiple active VDOMs. Both Active-Passive and Active-Active modes are supported. For every single VDOM we are able to configure a cluster, with a master and a slave unit. The network traffic that is directed to a certain cluster in a VDOM will stay inside this cluster. To keep the number of required interfaces as low as possible, the heartbeat interfaces configured for a VDOM are also used to keep the units in sync for all the clusters in the other VDOMs. Virtual clustering supports a load balancing mode called **VDOM partitioning**. The HA cluster will be configured as Active-Passive but we will have two or more virtual domains, with the primary and secondary node reversed (so that the unit that is primary for VDOM "A" is secondary for VDOM "B" and vice versa). We will be able to adjust the workload managing the configuration related to the single VDOM. If a failure occurs on a unit, all the network traffic will be moved to the surviving unit. Configuration steps for a cluster with VDOMs enabled are as follows:

1. Configure an Active-Passive cluster in the **System** pane as we have seen earlier in this chapter.
2. Enable VDOMs.
3. Create a new VDOM by navigating to the **System | VDOM** menu and select **Create New**.
4. Distribute the available interfaces between the various VDOMs by navigating to the **System | Network | Interface** menu.
5. Configure routing in the VDOMs.
6. After navigating to the **System | Config | HA** menu, we are able to move the clusters from one VDOM to another. The starting situation is shown in the following screenshot (we are working in a configuration containing the root domain and a VDOM called VDOMA):

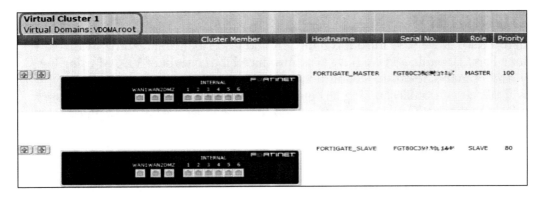

7. To balance the traffic, edit the MASTER. We will find a selection table called **VDOM partitioning** in which we are able to manage cluster membership in the different VDOMs.

8. Move the cluster to the VDOMA and modify the priority of the FortiGate units inside the clusters. Our result will be a VDOM partitioning shown as follows:

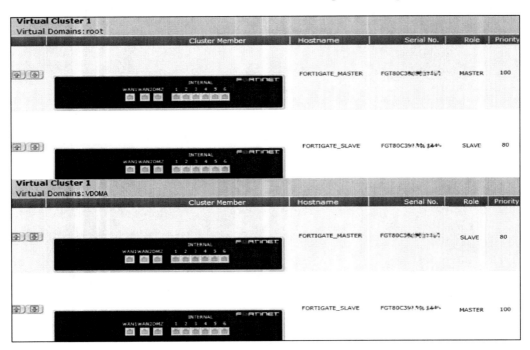

Summary

In this chapter we have introduced the HA and load balancing features available for a FortiGate unit, and we have also introduced the concept of VDOM using the virtual domains, to obtain an additional HA solution. In the next chapter we will talk about troubleshooting techniques that we need to know to manage errors related to the FortiGate configurations and functionalities we have explained in the previous chapters.

5
Troubleshooting

As seen earlier in *Chapter 1*, *First Steps*, a FortiGate unit is a UTM device. However, we also know that the appliance, in addition to the security features, has comprehensive capabilities for VLAN management, routing, VPNs, and high availability. Troubleshooting a FortiGate requires a structured approach to locate which one of the different levels or features is triggering the problem. To make the explanation easier, we will divide troubleshooting into five general areas:

- Routing
- Security policies and profiles
- Virtual domains
- VPN
- High Availability

In this chapter we will focus on diagnostic tools that are (for the most part) based on the CLI. To troubleshoot the aforementioned five areas, we will start from a group of tools dedicated to hardware diagnostics, then we will see a group of commands to identify errors related to layers 2 and 3 of the TCP/IP stack and a group of diagnostic controls focused on the higher level features.

Base system diagnostics

The status screen in the web-based manager includes a high level overview of information such as the system time (that is important, for example, to have coherent error messages and log recording), CPU and memory usage, license information, and alerts, as we can see in the following screenshot:

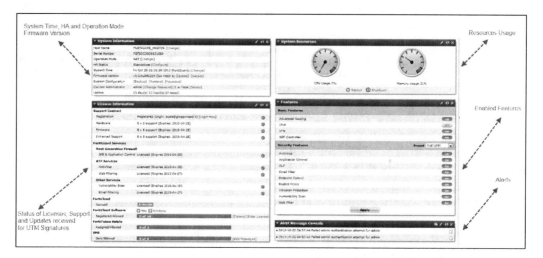

Although this screen is useful for a rapid assessment of the situation, our diagnostic tools usually have to dig deeper. The first base command we will use in the CLI is get system. This command can open more than eighty information options, dedicated to the different features of the FortiGate units. Among the others, we are able to check counters related to performance, such as:

- Startup configuration errors with the get system startup-error-log command.

- Firewall traffic statistics related to the traffic with the get system performance firewall statistics command.

- Firewall packet distribution statistics with the get system performance firewall packet-distribution command.

- Information about the most intensive CPU processes with the get system performance top, that will show a screen divided in columns, as we can see in the following screenshot:

```
Run Time:  13 days, 13 hours and 29 minutes
0U, 0S, 100I; 502T, 317F, 85KF
            httpsd      549        S      0.3      2.9
            httpsd       96        S      0.1      3.4
            pyfcgid     543        S      0.0      3.9
            pyfcgid     540        S      0.0      3.8
```

Another fundamental command we will use is `diagnose hardware`, which is used for problem-solving procedures related to certificates, devices, PCI, and system information. The devices menu is opened with the `diagnose hardware deviceinfo`, and includes a `disk` option to recover information about internal disks (if present) and a `nic` option to display data from network interfaces. The latter also shows on screen the errors and the drops related to network packets, as we can see in the following screenshot:

```
FORTIGATE_MASTER # diagnose hardware deviceinfo nic
The following NICs are available:
        dmz
        eth0
        internal
        wan1
        wan2

FORTIGATE_MASTER # diagnose hardware deviceinfo nic wan1

System_Device_Name            wan1
Current_HWaddr                00:09:0f:ce:f4:9a
Permanent_HWaddr              00:09:0f:ce:f4:9a

Link                          up
Speed                         100
Duplex                        full
State                         up(0x1203)
MTU_Size                      1500
Rx_Length_Errors              0
Rx_Over_Errors        0
Rx_CRC_Errors                 0
Rx_Frame_Errors               0
Rx_FIFO_Errors                0
```

To have access to real-time information, we will use the `diagnose debug` command. The `diagnose debug report` is not a troubleshooting tool, but is used to create a report for the Fortinet technical support. We will talk about additional options for the `diagnose debug` command later, in relation to TCP/IP debugging.

Troubleshooting routing

The tools that we will see in the following paragraphs will be required to troubleshoot the addressing and routing features of the TCP/IP protocol. Before we proceed to explain the single tools and commands for troubleshooting, we can take advantage of a real-world suggestion. In order to perform the troubleshooting steps in a more comfortable way, it is often advisable to use a client for SSH and Telnet such as PuTTY (`http://bit.ly/1kyS98`), to launch two separate sessions on a FortiGate unit. One of the two consoles will be dedicated to watch the results of the debug commands. The second console will be dedicated to launch commands, such as ping and traceroute that we will use to trigger actions that will be visible in the first open console. In the following screenshot we have a `diagnose sniffer packet port1 icmp` command running on the session opened to the left-hand side and an `execute ping` command on the session opened on the right-hand side window:

Layer 2 and layer 3 TCP/IP diagnostics

In *Chapter 4, High Availability*, while talking about Virtual MAC addresses, we explained the importance of the ARP cache to resolve devices to their IP address. Some issues can be solved only by correcting the ARP table that associates IP and MAC addresses. The `diagnose ip arp list` command shows the ARP cache as shown in the following screenshot:

```
FORTIGATE_MASTER # diagnose ip arp list
index=21 ifname=VPNPC 0.0.0.0  state=00000040 use=84190740 confirm=84196740 update=84190740 ref=1
index=4 ifname=wan1 151.22.6.129 00:0f:e2:c4:78:85 state=00000002 use=0 confirm=55 update=473 ref=13
```

The following commands are used to manage the ARP cache:

* The `execute clear system arp table` command to remove the ARP cache.

- The `diagnose ip arp delete <interface name> <IP address>` command to remove a single ARP entry.

- The `diagnose ip arp flush <interface name>` command to remove all entries associated with a single interface.

- The `config system arp-table` command to add a static ARP entry. This command requires two further commands:

    ° The `config system arp-table` command

    ° The `edit` command to create a new entry and to modify an existing entry or to create a new one

- Three mandatory parameters are:

    ° `set mac`, to configure a MAC address for the entry

    ° `set ip`, to configure an IP address for the entry

    ° `set interface`, to select the interface that is connected to the MAC and IP

In the following screenshot we can see all the required steps to add the entry number 3 on our ARP cache with the following parameters: ip `192.168.12.1` with a mac `F0:DE:F1:E4:75:B9` on the internal interface:

```
FORTIGATE_MASTER # config system arp-table

FORTIGATE_MASTER (arp-table) # edit 3
new entry '3' added

FORTIGATE_MASTER (3) # set ip 192.168.12.1

FORTIGATE_MASTER (3) # set mac F0:DE:F1:E4:75:B9

FORTIGATE_MASTER (3) # set interface internal

FORTIGATE_MASTER (3) # end
```

The use of a static ARP entry can be useful, for example, to resolve and prevent problems such as ARP poisoning. For more information you can read the article from *Corey Nachreiner*: **Anatomy of an ARP Poisoning Attack** available at
http://www.watchguard.com/infocenter/editorial/135324. asp.

We can now take care of layer 3, especially from the point of view of routing. As in any device that manages networking, the most used command (included in the ICMP protocol) is the ping command. A FortiGate unit supports two kinds of ping commands: `execute ping <IP address>` and a command dedicated to modify the behavior of the ping command, `execute ping-options`, that includes parameters such as:

- `data-size`: To select the datagram size in bytes (between 0 and 65507)
- `interval`: To set a value in seconds between two pings
- `repeat-count`: To select the number of pings to send
- `source`: To specify a source interface (default value is auto-select)
- `view-settings`: Used to show the current ping options
- `timeout`: To specify time out in seconds

In the following screenshot we have modified some ping parameters and verified them with the `view-settings` parameter:

```
FORTIGATE_MASTER # execute ping-options interval 10

FORTIGATE_MASTER # execute ping-options data-size 30000

FORTIGATE_MASTER # execute ping-options timeout 10

FORTIGATE_MASTER # execute ping-options view-settings
Ping Options:
        Repeat Count: 5
        Data Size: 30000
        Timeout: 10
        Interval: 10
        TTL: 64
        TOS: 0
        DF bit: unset
        Source Address: auto
        Pattern:
        Pattern Size in Bytes: 0
        Validate Reply: no

FORTIGATE_MASTER #
```

Another fundamental command, based on ICMP is `execute traceroute <dest>`, that allows us to see all the hops (networking devices) that a network packet traverses, starting from the FortiGate to a destination (which can be an IP address or an FQDN). Having the full path shown can be important to detect a wrong or faulty hop along the path. The usefulness of traceroute is related to how many devices along the route allow the use of the ICMP protocol, but also if we use it only inside to troubleshoot our internal corporate network, the results of this simple command are extremely useful. To show the result of a traceroute and have fun along the way, we can use the so called "Star Wars Traceroute"; `execute traceroute 216.81.59.173`, that will show the opening crawl to Star Wars Episode IV (a result that was obtained making clever use of hostnames and routing). We can see a (small) part of the result in the following screenshot:

```
12  206.214.251.1 <Episode.IV>  179.979 ms  178.294 ms  178.888 ms
13  206.214.251.6 <A.NEW.HOPE>  178.475 ms  179.073 ms  180.857 ms
14  206.214.251.9 <It.is.a.period.of.civil.war>  179.480 ms  179.908 ms  179.735 ms
15  206.214.251.14 <Rebel.spaceships>  179.506 ms  180.401 ms  182.422 ms
16  206.214.251.17 <striking.from.a.hidden.base>  178.955 ms  179.517 ms  180.215 ms
17  206.214.251.22 <have.won.their.first.victory>  181.174 ms  183.257 ms  178.804 ms
18  206.214.251.25 <against.the.evil.Galactic.Empire>  178.301 ms  178.297 ms  178.177 ms
19  206.214.251.30 <During.the.battle>  185.664 ms  180.529 ms  181.305 ms
20  206.214.251.33 <Rebel.spies.managed>  181.168 ms  181.053 ms  180.056 ms
21  206.214.251.38 <to.steal.secret.plans>  178.677 ms  179.328 ms  179.126 ms
22  206.214.251.41 <to.the.Empires.ultimate.weapon>  181.104 ms  180.224 ms  182.475 ms
23  206.214.251.46 <the.DEATH.STAR>  179.609 ms  178.836 ms  178.736 ms
24  206.214.251.49 <an.armored.space.station>  178.978 ms  180.202 ms  179.609 ms
25  206.214.251.54 <with.enough.power.to>  181.348 ms  193.832 ms  179.860 ms
26  206.214.251.57 <destroy.an.entire.planet>  179.103 ms  178.947 ms  178.624 ms
```

The next logical step to debug problems at layer 3 of TCP/IP is to verify the routing table, something that we are able to do with the `get router info routing-table all` command. The resulting information text could be very lengthy, so we are able to filter the output using the parameters including:

- `details`: Show routing table details information
- `rip`: Show RIP routing table
- `ospf`: Show OSPF routing table
- `isis`: Show ISIS routing table
- `static`: Show static routing table
- `connected`: Show connected routing table
- `database`: Show routing information base

The routing table shows the routing entries and their origin (the routing protocol that added an entry in the routing table).

Troubleshooting security policies and profiles

Fixing errors generated by a security policy requires tools to verify the network traffic flow, including verifications of protocols and ports. The following CLI tools are fundamental to troubleshooting issues related to security filters.

FortiOS packet sniffer

All FortiGate units have a built-in packet sniffer (or network analyser, a feature that captures all the data packets that pass through a given network interface or device). The packet sniffer includes six levels of information numbered from verbose 1 (basic information) to verbose 6 (that incorporates a lot of information also regarding the interfaces).

The command to use is:

- `diagnose sniffer packet`. The parameters are:
    - ◦ `<interface>`: A specific network interface to sniff or "any"
    - ◦ `<filter>`: A logical filter (or none to process all the network traffic)
    - ◦ `<verbose>`: A value from 1 to 6 to define how much information we will see
    - ◦ `<count>`: Number of packets to catch before stopping

In the following screenshot we have used the `diagnose sniffer packet wan1 tcp and port 443` command to see packets passing through our `wan1` interface (IP address 151.22.6.188) on port `443` (the form in the diagnose log is 151.22.6.188.443). On the other side we have a couple of sessions, on port 19937 and 19938 from 95.246.181.172.

```
FORTIGATE_MASTER # diagnose sniffer packet wan1 tcp and port 443
interfaces=[wan1]
filters=[tcp]
0.909854 151.22.6.188.443 -> 95.246.181.172.19937: psh 2168517239 ack 1888039049
1.009969 95.246.181.172.19937 -> 151.22.6.188.443: psh 1888039049 ack 2168517868
1.014160 151.22.6.188.443 -> 95.246.181.172.19937: psh 2168517868 ack 1888040094
1.060814 95.246.181.172.19938 -> 151.22.6.188.443: ack 50617913
1.126032 95.246.181.172.19937 -> 151.22.6.188.443: psh 1888040094 ack 2168518689
1.130084 151.22.6.188.443 -> 95.246.181.172.19937: psh 2168518689 ack 1888041139
1.238092 95.246.181.172.19937 -> 151.22.6.188.443: psh 1888041139 ack 2168519542
1.242096 151.22.6.188.443 -> 95.246.181.172.19937: psh 2168519542 ack 1888042184
1.353904 95.246.181.172.19937 -> 151.22.6.188.443: psh 1888042184 ack 2168520331
1.357917 151.22.6.188.443 -> 95.246.181.172.19937: psh 2168520331 ack 1888043229
1.469715 95.246.181.172.19937 -> 151.22.6.188.443: psh 1888043229 ack 2168521120
1.473727 151.22.6.188.443 -> 95.246.181.172.19937: psh 2168521120 ack 1888044274
1.473766 151.22.6.188.443 -> 95.246.181.172.19937: fin 2168521877 ack 1888044274
1.549045 95.246.181.172.19937 -> 151.22.6.188.443: fin 1888044274 ack 2168521877
1.549108 151.22.6.188.443 -> 95.246.181.172.19937: ack 1888044275
1.565535 95.246.181.172.19937 -> 151.22.6.188.443: ack 2168521878
1.594018 95.246.181.172.19938 -> 151.22.6.188.443: psh 559680753 ack 50617913
1.598022 151.22.6.188.443 -> 95.246.181.172.19938: psh 50617913 ack 559681798
```

 Other Fortinet products, such as FortiAnalyzer, FortiMail, and FortiManager also provide the CLI packet sniffer.

Some units that have **Network Processors (NPU)** will only show the initial packets of a session. On a smaller unit the NPU can be disabled to show all packets of a connection. The same can be done on larger units as well and some of them have a command to enable packet captures even with the NPU enabled:

`diagnose npu nplite fastpath disable`

The thing to remember is that NPU offload provides a significant performance increase. Disabling the NPU fastpath could potentially lead to performance problems on heavily loaded firewalls.

Network traffic should enter an interface and find a way to go out from the FortiGate unit. To verify that the flow of data is moving in the right manner, we are able to use the command `diagnose debug flow filter`, using the available parameters that include:

- `addr`: IP address
- `daddr`: Destination IP address
- `dport`: Destination port
- `port`: Port
- `proto`: Protocol number
- `saddr`: Source IP address
- `sport`: Source port

Two additional commands: `diagnose debug flow show console enable` and `diagnose debug flow trace start`, are required show data in the CLI.

The suggested steps to use the packet sniffer are the ones in the following document **How to use debug flow to filter traffic** in the Fortinet Knowledge Base at `http://bit.ly/HkuLuz`. In the following table we are able to see some options for the diagnose debug command:

`diagnose debug disable`	To start from a clean debug situation
`diagnose debug flow trace stop`	Stop the trace of debugging
`diagnose debug flow filter clear`	To clear all filters
`diagnose debug reset`	Reset all debug commands
`diagnose debug flow filter addr x.y.z.k`	Filter to see only address x.y.z.k
`diagnose debug flow show console enable`	Display the trace on console
`diagnose debug flow show function-name enable`	Show function name
`diagnose debug console timestamp enable`	Put the time in the debug
`diagnose debug flow trace start 999`	Start the trace of debugging
`diagnose debug enable`	Enable the debug command

To try the aforementioned list of actions, we will apply the procedure to verify traffic coming to our FortiGate unit from the IP address 78.13.250.37. First four commands will be used to clear our debug parameters, as shown in the following screenshot:

```
FORTIGATE_MASTER # diagnose debug disable

FORTIGATE_MASTER # diagnose debug flow trace stop

FORTIGATE_MASTER # diagnose debug flow filter clear

FORTIGATE_MASTER # diagnose debug reset
```

Then we will set the debug flow parameters as required. The commands we used are the ones we can see in the following screenshot:

```
FORTIGATE_MASTER # diagnose debug flow filter addr 78.13.250.37

FORTIGATE_MASTER # diagnose debug flow show console
do not show trace messages on console

FORTIGATE_MASTER # diagnose debug flow show function-name enable
show function name

FORTIGATE_MASTER # diagnose debug console timestamp
console timestamp is enable.
FORTIGATE_MASTER # diagnose debug flow trace start 10
```

Firewall session lists information

We have tools in the web-based manager to verify the status of the firewall feature on a FortiGate unit and to retrieve data about firewall sessions, starting from the three menus in the **System pane**, **Top Sources**, **Top Destinations**, and **Top Applications**, shown in the following screenshot:

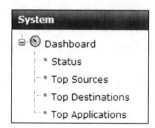

 To show the active sessions, packets, and bytes we have an additional tool, the Policy Monitor which is available by navigating to the **Policy | Monitors | Policy Monitor** menu.

If we need to dig deeper in the firewall session information, we have to use the CLI command, `diagnose sys session`. Some base parameters are:

- `clear`: Clear a specific filter or reset all the previously configured filters
- `filter`: List session with filters
- `full-stat`: Fully stat session
- `list`: List sessions
- `stat`: Stat session

For example, let's launch the command `diagnose sys session stat`. We will receive a quick overview of the firewall sessions, in the format we can see in the following screenshot:

```
FORTIGATE_MASTER # diagnose sys session stat
misc info:      session_count=4 setup_rate=0 exp_count=0 clash=0
                memory_tension_drop=0 ephemeral=0/32768 removeable=0  ha_scan=0
delete=0, flush=0, dev_down=0/0
TCP sessions:
                2 in ESTABLISHED state
firewall error stat:
error1=00000000
error2=00000000
error3=00000000
error4=00000000
tt=00000000
cont=00000000
ids_recv=00000000
url_recv=00000000
av_recv=00000000
fqdn_count=00000000
tcp reset stat:
                syncqf=0 acceptqf=0 no-listener=334 data=0 ses=0 ips=0
global: ses_limit=0 ses6_limit=0 rt_limit=0 rt6_limit=0
```

To see a detailed list, we will launch the `diagnose sys session list` command. The resulting output will list the existing sessions with detailed information including protocol status and traffic information as shown in the following screenshot:

```
session info: proto=6 proto_state=01 duration=2 expire=3600 timeout=3600 flags=00000000 sockflag=00000000 sockport=0 av_idx=0 use=3
origin-shaper=
reply-shaper=
per_ip_shaper=
ha_id=0 policy_dir=0 tunnel=/
state=log local may_dirty
statistic(bytes/packets/allow_err): org=6394/11/1 reply=3614/9/1 tuples=2
orgin->sink: org pre->in, reply out->post dev=4->7/7->4 gwy=151.22.6.188/0.0.0.0
hook=pre dir=org act=noop 94.37.242.43:63243->151.22.6.188:443(0.0.0.0:0)
hook=post dir=reply act=noop 151.22.6.188:443->94.37.242.43:63243(0.0.0.0:0)
pos/(before,after) 0/(0,0), 0/(0,0)
misc=0 policy_id=0 id_policy_id=0 auth_info=0 chk_client_info=0 vd=0
serial=000035f9 tos=ff/ff ips_view=0 app_list=0 app=0
dd_type=0 dd_mode=0
per_ip_bandwidth meter: addr=94.37.242.43, bps=7875
```

For a more complete explanation of the `diagnose sys session` command, please refer to the document **Troubleshooting Tip: FortiGate Firewall session list information** in the Fortinet Knowledge base at `http://bit.ly/1eXMymK`.

Debugging URL and anti-spam filters

A common issue with URL and anti-spam filters is to understand why a specific filter or rule is blocking (or not blocking) a defined website or content. To debug the URL filters we have configured for a single address (or for a whole category), we can use the `diagnose debug application urlfilter <debug level>` command. To identify a word that is matched by a filter, we will use the `diagnose webfilter bword matchfilter <logstring>` command (`<logstring>` is the group of numbers read from the end of the log entry). The `diagnose webfilter fortiguard statistics list` command will show rating statistics. A similar method will be used for anti-spam issues. The first command to use is `diagnose debug application spamfilter <debug level>`. The `diagnose spamfilter bword matchfilter <logstring>` command identifies a word that is matched by an anti-spam filter.

Troubleshooting virtual domains

In addition to the troubleshooting techniques we have talked about in the previous sections, virtual domains have some peculiar aspects that we need to understand if we are required to solve an issue. We have to consider a series of hardware limits when we define how many VDOMs we are able to configure on a single FortiGate unit. If the device becomes overloaded, we can experience slow performing or non-responsive VDOMs. This kind of problem can be defined looking at the resource usage. We are able to define minimum levels of resources when using virtual domains, so that each one has access to the resources it needs. Resource settings are based on global settings or on a per-VDOM configuration.

 An important document to consider for the virtual domains is the **FortiGate Maximum Values Table for FortiOS 5.0** available at `http://docs.fortinet.com/fgt/handbook/50/fortigate-max-values-50.pdf`, that defines upper limits for a large part the FortiGate features, including VDOMs.

The remaining problems are usually solved using the built-in sniffer and the firewall session diagnostics.

Troubleshooting VPN

With the tools we have explained, we are able to troubleshoot VPN connections. We can start with SSL VPN debugging and follow the steps suggested in the **Debugging FortiGate configurations** document (http://docs.fortinet.com/cb/ html/index.html#page/FOS_Cookbook/Install_advanced/cb_ts_debug.html). The steps are as follows:

1. Verify the current debug configuration with the `diagnose debug info` command.

2. Display debug messages for SSL VPN using the `diagnose debug application sslvpn -1` command.

3. Use `diagnose debug enable` to display debug messages.

Any error will be shown on screen. To debug an IPSEC site-to-site VPN connection, a good list of steps is the one posted by *Yuri Slobodyanyuk* in his blog: http://bit.ly/hzREm1. The steps are as follows:

1. Open an SSH session on the FortiGate unit.

2. Execute `diagnose debug enable` to enable debugging.

3. Execute `diagnose debug app ike -1` to verify IKE errors.

4. Execute `diagnose sniffer packet any <IP of the remote LAN>` to activate packet sniffing.

5. Open a second SSH session on the FortiGate unit.

6. Execute `exec ping-options source <IP of the local LAN interface>` to make the ping originate from the local network interface.

7. Execute `exec ping <IP of the remote LAN>` to bring up the VPN connection.

8. Go back to the SSH session opened at step 1 and verify if errors are shown.

Talking about VPN connection, it is important to check the status of our digital certificates. Navigate to the **System | Certificates** menu. Here we have information about our locally configured SSL certificates (as shown in the following screenshot) in the **Local Certificates** pane and additional menus to verify remotely released certificates, such as CA certificates and the CRL (certificate revocation list).

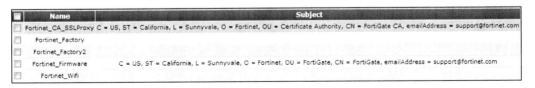

Troubleshooting High Availability (HA)

Talking about high availability, we are able to divide this topic into two different aspects:

- Troubleshooting HA clusters
- Troubleshooting virtual clustering

Troubleshooting HA clusters

We can begin troubleshooting an HA cluster using the following steps:

1. Apply a minimal security policy that allows to send traffic through the cluster and verify that the connection is working.
2. We have to create a continuous network traffic through the cluster and then we can try to shut down the primary unit.
3. Network traffic should flow with no interruption.
4. Now we are able to restart the primary unit.
5. We have to check the configuration on the FortiGate devices, to verify that it is the same on all the cluster units.
6. Next step is to verify that all the interfaces are up and connected as required by the configuration.

Additional things to consider when troubleshooting an HA cluster are related to the risks of a split-brain scenario. The split-brain syndrome may occur when all of the heartbeat links go down simultaneously, with the cluster units still running. Each FortiGate unit could believe itself to be the only one running, a situation that creates issues on the connections and incongruent configuration data. In this case we should:

- Verify that the devices between the two cluster units, along the connection dedicated to the heartbeat, do not block cluster HA heartbeat communication.
- Avoid overloading the cluster units because a slow exchange of heartbeat packets could create a split-brain. If it is not possible to reduce the workload, we are able to modify the heartbeat timing. The command to use is `config system ha set hb-interval <interval_integer>`.

Another type of issue that we may encounter while using an HA cluster is related to slow replacement of faulty nodes. Suggested steps to face such a scenario include:

- Increasing the number of gratuitous ARP packets sent; this will reduce the failover time. We can use the `config system ha` command followed by the `set arps 20` parameter (maximum supported value is 60, while the default value is 8 packets). Another parameter that should be changed is the time interval in seconds between gratuitous ARP packets. The default setting of 8 seconds can be modified to, for example, 5 seconds, using the `config system ha` command in the CLI followed by the parameter `set arps-interval 5`.

- On some HA links, a feature called subsecond failover is supported, to reduce the failover time to less than a second. The system will not wait for the monitoring function to poll the interfaces, but a link failure system call will be sent as soon as a monitored interface goes offline, to initiate a failover. This operational mode requires interfaces that support the link failure system call.

Troubleshooting virtual clustering

The suggestions we have seen for troubleshooting HA clusters do apply also for virtual clusters. However, there are some additional steps we can take to troubleshoot this HA configuration:

1. Log into each VDOM and verify that the cluster is working as expected for that specific VDOM, using the `get system status` command and the packet sniffer we have seen in previous sections.

2. Verify that the traffic is moving through the expected cluster unit, using data flow verification tools and the unit statistics (both from the web-based manager and from the CLI).

Summary

In this chapter, we have seen some troubleshooting techniques and tools to resolve problems in five main areas of a FortiGate unit (routing, security policies and profiles, virtual domains, VPN, and high availability). We have examined the available commands and options to resolve issues with FortiGate services, because in troubleshooting, the use of CLI is almost mandatory.

Index

Symbols

M

Managed client 47
Move To option 24

N

network
   about 29
   Directly connected networks 22
   remote networks 22
Network Address Translation (NAT) mode
      12
Network Processors (NPU) 94

O

One-time schedule 37
Open Shortest Path First. *See* OSPF
operation mode
   selecting 12-15
OSPF
   about 26, 27
   configuring, on Fortigate 27
   routes, monitoring 29
OSPF area 28, 29
ospf parameter 93
OSPF router ID 27, 28

P

Password parameter 76
Per-IP shaping 45
policy
   configuring, for SSL VPN portal 58
policy-based VPN 60
policy routing 23, 24
port 36
port parameter 95
profiles
   troubleshooting 93
protocol numbers
   URL 24
proto parameter 95
PuTTY
   URL 90

Q

QOS (Quality of Service) 45

R

recurring schedule 37
Remote Authentication Dial in User Service
      (RADIUS) 69
remote networks 22
repeat-count parameter 92
rip parameter 93
route-based VPN 60
routing
   Layer 2 diagnostics 90-93
   layer 3 diagnostics 90-93
   troubleshooting 90
routing protocols
   exterior routing protocols 25
   interior routing protocols 25

S

saddr parameter 95
schedules
   about 37, 38
   One-time schedule 37
SCTP 36
Secure Sockets Layer (SSL) 52
security association (SA) 62
security policies
   about 45, 46
   troubleshooting 93
services
   updating 17, 18
services, Firewall 35, 36
session-sync command 79
set interface parameter 91
set ip parameter 91
set mac parameter 91
set peerip <peer_ipv4> 79
Shared policy shaping 45
software switch 20
source parameter 92
sport parameter 95

W

web-based manager
  configuring 9
web content filtering 43
web filtering 42, 43
web-only mode
  about 53

SSL VPN portal, using with 53
web script filtering 43

Z

zones 56
zones, Firewall 33, 34

Thank you for buying
Getting Started with FortiGate

About Packt Publishing

Packt, pronounced 'packed', published its first book "Mastering phpMyAdmin for Effective MySQL Management" in April 2004 and subsequently continued to specialize in publishing highly focused books on specific technologies and solutions.

Our books and publications share the experiences of your fellow IT professionals in adapting and customizing today's systems, applications, and frameworks. Our solution based books give you the knowledge and power to customize the software and technologies you're using to get the job done. Packt books are more specific and less general than the IT books you have seen in the past. Our unique business model allows us to bring you more focused information, giving you more of what you need to know, and less of what you don't.

Packt is a modern, yet unique publishing company, which focuses on producing quality, cutting-edge books for communities of developers, administrators, and newbies alike. For more information, please visit our website: www.packtpub.com.

About Packt Enterprise

In 2010, Packt launched two new brands, Packt Enterprise and Packt Open Source, in order to continue its focus on specialization. This book is part of the Packt Enterprise brand, home to books published on enterprise software – software created by major vendors, including (but not limited to) IBM, Microsoft and Oracle, often for use in other corporations. Its titles will offer information relevant to a range of users of this software, including administrators, developers, architects, and end users.

Writing for Packt

We welcome all inquiries from people who are interested in authoring. Book proposals should be sent to author@packtpub.com. If your book idea is still at an early stage and you would like to discuss it first before writing a formal book proposal, contact us; one of our commissioning editors will get in touch with you.

We're not just looking for published authors; if you have strong technical skills but no writing experience, our experienced editors can help you develop a writing career, or simply get some additional reward for your expertise.

BackTrack - Testing Wireless Network Security

ISBN: 978-1-78216-406-7   Paperback: 108 pages

Secure yout wireless networks against attacks, hacks, and intruders with this step-by-step guide

1.   Make your wireless networks bulletproof

2.   Easily secure your network from intruders

3.   See how the hackers do it and learn how to defend yourself

Network Analysis using Wireshark Cookbook

ISBN: 978-1-84951-764-5   Paperback: 385 pages

110 recipes to analyze and troubleshoot network problems using Wireshark

1.   Place Wireshark in your network and configure it for effective network analysis

2.   Configure capture and display filters to get the required data

3.   Use Wireshark's powerful statistical tools to analyze your network and its expert system to pinpoint network problems

Please check **www.PacktPub.com** for information on our titles

Software Defined Networking with OpenFlow

ISBN: 978-1-84969-872-6   Paperback: 152 pages

Get hands-on with the platforms and debugging tools used to develop OpenFlow network control applications

1. Get to grips with the essentials of OpenFlow and its ecosystem features

2. Thorough overview of OpenSource switches, controllers, and tools

3. Build your own laboratory and develop your own networking apps

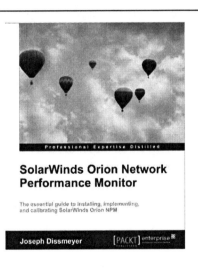

SolarWinds Orion Network Performance Monitor

ISBN: 978-1-84968-848-2   Paperback: 336 pages

The essential guide to installing, implementing, and calibrating SolarWinds Orion NPM

1. Master wireless monitoring and the control of wireless access points

2. Learn how to respond quickly and efficiently to network issues with SolarWinds Orion NPM

3. Build impressive reports to effectively visualize issues, solutions, and the overall health of your network

Please check **www.PacktPub.com** for information on our titles

Lightning Source UK Ltd.
Milton Keynes UK
UKOW02f2350261113

221875UK00002B/60/P